THE ECLOGUES

牧歌集

Also by Simon M. Yiyang

The Georgics: a Chinese translation
The Marriage Ritual: a logical novel

The Eclogues

a Chinese translation

Vergil

维吉尔

牧歌集

拉汉对照

Simon M. Yiyang 译注

First Edition MMXXIII

Published by Hyperimmune Books
Suwanee, GA, United States

PB ISBN: 979-8-9867759-2-0

HB ISBN: 979-8-9867759-3-7

1 2 1 2 1 2 1 2 7 7 7 7 7 7 7 7 7 3

arvo, bovi, sub tibi, Tityre, tegmine fagi.

献给牧场，献给牛羊；
献给你，Tityrus：
给你在榉树下的时光。

About the Author

Publius Vergilius Maro, commonly known as Vergil, is a poet in Rome during its profound transition from a republic to an empire.

His everlasting works *the Eclogues, the Georgics* and *the Aeneid* have deeply rooted in the entire Western civilization ever since his own time.

He is a master of Latin literature, a lover of Muse and the poet of the Iron Age.

———————∽०ᑕ✷ᗋ०⊂———————

About the Translator

Simon M. Yiyang is a logician from Serica, according to the author. He and his family are now living in Georgia, USA.

He also translated *the Georgics* into Chinese, which happened totally by accident. Well, he currently has no plans to translate *the Aeneid* — the author loved this work so much that he ordered the draft to be burnt due to even the tiniest imperfections.

ECLOGA I

　　牧人Meliboeus被迫流离，而Tityrus却刚获得自由身份，在榉树的华盖下悠闲地吹着芦笛；时代给人们带来了截然不同的命运。

ECLOGA I

M.   Tityre[1], tu patulae recubans sub tegmine fagi
     silvestrem tenui Musam[2] meditaris avena[3];
     nos patriae fines et dulcia linquimus arva.
     nos patriam fugimus; tu, Tityre, lentus in umbra
5   formosam resonare doces Amaryllida[4] silvas.

T.   o Meliboee, deus nobis haec otia fecit.
     namque erit ille mihi semper deus; illius aram
     saepe tener nostris ab ovilibus imbuet agnus.
     ille meas errare boves, ut cernis, et ipsum
10   ludere, quae vellem, calamo permisit agresti.

M.   non equidem invideo; miror magis: undique totis
     usque adeo turbatur agris. en, ipse capellas
     protinus aeger[5] ago; hanc etiam vix, Tityre, duco:

---

[1]Tityrus和Meliboeus应该是两位牧人，其中Meliboeus的田地被政府强征，所以流离失所。

[2]Muse是司掌音乐与诗歌的文艺女神，这里指代牧笛吹奏的歌曲。

[3]avena本是燕麦或者野燕麦，这里指代用空心的植物茎秆制成的牧笛。

[4]Amaryllis是一个女子的名字。而*formosa Amaryllis*大概是一首赞扬女孩子美丽的歌。

[5]aeger可能指Meliboeus自己染病在身，更可能指的是因为失去土地而伤心过度。

牧歌·其一

M.   Tityrus啊，
     你在榉树的华盖下闲躺，
     倾心于牧笛的细长，
     沉浸于山林的乐章；
     我们却要离开家乡，
     离开这甜美的农场。
     我们逃离家园，而你，Tityrus，
     你在这树荫下乘凉，
     你教会这大树歌唱，
     "美丽的Amaryllis"，在林间回响。

T.   噢，Meliboeus啊，
     是神明恩赐我们这等悠闲。
     我对他的虔诚将永远不变，
     而在他的祭坛边，
     也永远有我家的羊羔进献。
     如你所见，
     承其恩惠，我的牛群在游荡闲散，
     如我所愿，
     我自己也能将这乡野的牧笛把玩。

M.   我可不是嫉妒于你，更多则是惊叹：
     所有的田地，到处都是无尽的混乱。
     你看，我忍受这般凄苦，
     却要继续赶着羊群上路；
     而这头，Tityrus，眼看要跟不上脚步：

hic inter densas corylos modo namque gemellos,
15   spem gregis, ah, silice in nuda conixa reliquit.
      saepe malum hoc nobis, si mens non laeva fuisset,
      de caelo tactas memini praedicere quercus[1],
      [saepe sinistra cava praedixit ab ilice cornix.][2]
      sed tamen iste deus qui sit, da, Tityre, nobis.

20 **T.** urbem, quam dicunt Romam, Meliboee, putavi
        stultus ego huic nostrae similem, quo saepe solemus
        pastores ovium teneros depellere fetus:
        sic canibus catulos similis, sic matribus haedos
        noram, sic parvis componere magna solebam:
25   verum haec tantum alias inter caput extulit urbes,
        quantum lenta solent inter viburna[3] cupressi[4].

M. et quae tanta fuit Romam tibi causa videndi?

T. libertas[5], quae sera, tamen respexit inertem,
      candidior postquam tondenti barba cadebat;

---

[1]quercus可以特指是希腊Dodona圣林里的橡树。这橡树本是神王*Zeus*（即Juppiter，掌管闪电）的圣树，现在却被闪电击中，的确是大凶之兆。

[2]很多版本没有此行。

[3]viburna指Viburnum lantana，一种低矮的灌木，属于荚蒾属，经常作为观赏植物在路边种植。

[4]这里的柏树是Cupressus sempervirens，一种地中海柏树，可以长到三十多米高。

[5]这里libertas应该是与奴隶身份对应的自由身。所以Tityrus之前是奴隶，老了终于获得自由身份，可以自行去罗马观光，而不需要主人给的理由或者任务。罗马有些奴隶可以攒钱给自己或是奴隶配偶赎身。

它刚在茂密的榛树林里产下双胞小羊，
那可是族群的希望，
哎，却被遗弃在光秃的山岩之上。
如果我的脑子有一丁点开窍，
早就该记起上天赐予的凶兆：
那被天打雷劈，橡树的警告，
那树洞中，不幸乌鸦的哀号。
不说这些，Tityrus，
这神祇是哪位，还请指教。

T. 噢，Meliboeus，
有一座都市，它叫罗马，
我曾经以为，哎，我可真是傻，
以为那罗马，
就比我们牧民去卖嫩羊羔的城镇稍大——
就像是羊羔跟它妈，
就像是大狗和狗娃，
我曾以为它们只是大小有差！
但那都市，拿去跟其他的城镇比上一比，
正如柏树，在柔弱的荚蒾丛中独自傲立。

M. 等下，你何故要去见那罗马？

T. 是姗姗来迟的自由之身，
终于垂怜我这慵懒之人，
而我那把剃刀上的白刃，
落下已然是更白的须根；

30   respexit tamen, et longo post tempore venit,
       postquam nos Amaryllis habet, Galatea[1] reliquit.
       namque, fatebor enim, dum me Galatea tenebat,
       nec spes libertatis erat, nec cura peculi.
       quamvis multa meis exiret victima saeptis,
35   pinguis et ingratae premeretur caseus urbi,
       non umquam gravis aere domum mihi dextra redibat.

M. mirabar, quid maesta deos, Amarylli, vocares,
       cui pendere sua patereris in arbore poma[2]:
       Tityrus hinc aberat[3]. ipsae te, Tityre, pinus,
40   ipsi te fontes, ipsa haec arbusta vocabant[4].

T. quid facerem? neque servitio me exire licebat,
       nec tam praesentis alibi cognoscere divos.

---

[1]这里Galatea应该是Tityrus之前的女主人，可能比较刻薄，所以看不到赎身的希望，而动词relinquo指的是女主人死后把奴隶给了Amaryllis。还有比较普遍的理解是，Tityrus之前喜欢的是Galatea，但她离他而去，所以后来他又喜欢上Amaryllis。

[2]poma可以指各种的果实。

[3]这里动词absum不是说Tityrus去罗马远行，而是他获得了自由身份，脱离了奴籍。

[4]这里的呼唤更多是形容获得自由身之后，感觉自然环境都一下子和蔼可亲了。

虽说它垂怜，但还是来得太迟——
那个Galatea已经逝去，
之后Amaryllis把我占据！
我需要承认，那时Galatea是我的主上，
我既看不到自由的希望，
更没有用心去照顾牛羊。
无论我从羊圈中拿出多少来敬神，
或是压榨多少美味的奶酪给城镇，
只是他们都不会感恩！
我每天回家时，那右手边，
永远没有多少沉甸的铜钱。

M. 我之前一直惊叹，
Amaryllis你为何郁郁寡欢，
为何事要将神明呼喊，
甘愿忍受果子在枝头腐烂[1]！
原来是Tityrus已经获得自由！
噢，Tityrus，
那劲松呼唤着你，
那清泉呼唤着你，
那果园呼唤着你！

T. 那时我又能做甚？
既没有办法可以赎身，
更不知别处哪有如此的善神！

---

[1]缺少奴隶干活了。

hic illum vidi iuvenem, Meliboee, quot annis

bis senos cui nostra dies altaria fumant.

45   hic mihi responsum primus dedit ille petenti:

'pascite, ut ante, boves, pueri, submittite[1] tauros.'

M. fortunate senex, ergo tua rura manebunt,

et tibi magna satis, quamvis lapis omnia nudus

limosoque palus obducat pascua iunco[2]!

50   non insueta gravis temptabunt pabula fetas,

nec mala vicini pecoris contagia laedent.

fortunate senex, hic, inter flumina nota

et fontis sacros, frigus captabis opacum!

hinc tibi, quae semper, vicino ab limite[3] saepes

55   Hyblaeis[4] apibus florem depasta salicti

saepe levi somnum suadebit inire susurro;

hinc alta sub rupe canet frondator[5] ad auras;

nec tamen interea raucae, tua cura, palumbes[6],

nec gemere aeria cessabit turtur[7] ab ulmo.

---

[1]这里summitto是说喂养耕牛，但不要宰杀的意思。

[2]iuncus指灯心草或者类似野草。

[3]limes指两块土地之间分割的小道。

[4]Hybla是Sicily的一座山，以鲜花与蜜蜂闻名。

[5]这是修剪葡萄叶和榆树叶的园丁，参见《农事诗》II.362-370。

[6]palumbes指Columba palumbus，欧洲的一种林鸽。

[7]turtur指Streptopelia turtur，欧洲斑鸠。

Meliboeus啊，于是我见到了那年轻人[1]，

我家祭坛每年要给他献上，

两个六日[2]的浓烟滚滚！

他也首先回应了我急切的请求：

"汝要照常喂牛，孩子们，不要宰杀耕牛。"

M.　你这幸运的老头，

可以把你的土地继续保有，

即使牧场上遍地是裸露的石丘，

即使沼泽泥泞，野草侵蚀游走，

那也让你衣食无忧！

陌生的草料就不会接触怀孕的母兽，

临近的兽群也不会传染恶毒的诅咒！

你这幸运的老头，

这神圣的泉水，这熟知的溪流，

你还能在荫凉下享受！

你的藩篱，与邻家的边界小道，

Hybla的蜜蜂，如同往常，

在那儿亲吻柳树的花香，

嗡嗡而轻柔的声响，

每每把你送入梦乡。

耸立的山岩旁，

葡萄园丁迎着微风，歌声嘹亮；

高大的榆树上，

你心头的林鸽发出空洞的声响，

而那斑鸠也在不停地低声鸣唱。

---

[1] 神明不老不死，所以看上去像是年轻人。

[2] 参见V.67，这里是一年两次的祭祀，不应该翻译成十二日。

60 **T.** ante leves ergo pascentur in aethere[1] cervi,
        et freta destituent nudos in litore pisces,
        ante pererratis amborum finibus exsul
        aut Ararim[2] Parthus[3] bibet, aut Germania[4] Tigrim[5],
        quam nostro illius labatur pectore voltus.

65 **M.** at nos hinc alii sitientis ibimus Afros[6],
        pars Scythiam[7] et rapidum Cretae[8] veniemus Oaxen[9],
        et penitus toto divisos orbe Britannos[10].
        en umquam patrios longo post tempore finis,
        pauperis et tuguri congestum caespite culmen,
70   post aliquot, mea regna, videns mirabor aristas?
        impius haec tam culta novalia[11] miles habebit,
        barbarus has segetes? en, quo discordia civis
        produxit miseros! his nos consevimus agros!

---

[1]有版本作aequore，水中。

[2]Arar河，又作Araris河，是Rhine河的支流，位于Germania领地西边，今France境内。

[3]Parthi人，生活在今Iran周围，汉人称之为安息，当时以弓术闻名。

[4]Germania是当时北方的蛮族。

[5]即Tigris河。

[6]Afer即非洲，当时又称为Libya。

[7]Scythia在罗马的东北，从黑海北岸一直延续到东欧平原，是当时所知的极北苦寒之地。

[8]Creta即Crete岛。一说指白垩石，存疑。

[9]Oaxes河，又称为Axus，河边有同名的城镇，都在Crete岛上。一说是遥远东方一条未知的河流。Crete岛上条件并不艰苦，存疑。

[10]Britanni即今Britain岛。

[11]也可以指休耕之田，见《农事诗》I.71-72。

T. 要等轻盈的雄鹿，
在空中吃草游牧，
或是等大海干枯，
把赤裸的鱼群留给大陆，
要等我们两头那些游民，
互相游荡到对方的老巢：
Parthi人在Arar河里洗澡[1]，
Germania人却在Tigris河边睡觉，
我才敢忘却那人[2]的容貌！

M. 如今我们一些人要去非洲，干渴的世界，
还有一部分要去Scythia，感受北风凛冽，
或是去Creta岛上，体验Oaxes河水肆虐，
甚至是那Britanni岛，与世隔绝！
啊，经年累月，
不知是否还能重回故乡，
看我可怜的农房，
屋顶上杂草猛长，
边上的农作物三三两两——
我本该是这土地的国王！
那无德的士兵占据了我的新田？
那粗鲁的蛮人侵吞了我的庄稼？
噢，为何把分歧带给苦难的公民？
我们本是在自己的田地上耕耘！

---

[1] 原文是"饮河"。
[2] 通常理解这里的神指的是原名Gaius Octavius，现在叫Gaius Julius Caesar，后来被尊称为Caesar Augustus的年轻人，即未来罗马帝国的第一任皇帝。但是也可以指某位正好路过罗马的神祇，比如VI.3提到的*Apollo*。

insere nunc, Meliboee, piros, pone ordine vitis.

75 ite meae, felix quondam pecus, ite capellae.

non ego vos posthac, viridi proiectus in antro,

dumosa pendere procul de rupe videbo;

carmina nulla canam; non, me pascente, capellae,

florentem cytisum[1] et salices carpetis amaras.

80 **T.** hic tamen hanc mecum poteras requiescere noctem

fronde super viridi: sunt nobis mitia poma[2],

castaneae molles, et pressi copia lactis;

et iam summa procul villarum culmina fumant,

maioresque cadunt altis de montibus umbrae.

---

[1]cytisus是一种三叶草或者苜蓿，可能指Medicago arborea，木本苜蓿，是重要的饲料植物。参见《农事诗》II.431,III.394。

[2]poma可以指各种果实。这里为了押韵译为樱桃。

Meliboeus啊[1]，你现在还要去嫁接梨子，
种下葡萄，还要保证整齐成行[2]！
走吧，我的羊，
之前你们是那么欢畅，
走吧，我的羊！
从今往后，
我再没法在鲜草繁茂的洞穴下乘凉，
看着你们在荆棘丛生的乱石中游荡；
我不再把这牧歌吟唱；
我的羊，你们再也吃不上，
柳条的苦涩，苜蓿的花香。

T. 不管怎样，今夜你可在此歇下脚，
跟我一起，在这绿叶床上睡一觉；
我们有香软的栗子和成熟的樱桃，
还有足够多，压制的乳酪；
看着远方农舍顶上炊烟袅袅，
大山的阴影渐渐将四周笼罩[3]。

---

[1]这句对自己说，应该是反话，就是"现在了还去接什么梨子，种什么葡萄"。
[2]参见《农事诗》II.274-288。
[3]原文是"阴影愈发变长"。

ECLOGA II

　　牧人Corydon疯狂地恋上了Alexis，但是后者似乎并不领情。Corydon当然也有另外的选择，但我爱的人不爱我，这永远是人世间最真实的爱情故事。

ECLOGA II

Formosum pastor Corydon[1] ardebat Alexim,
delicias domini, nec quid speraret habebat;
tantum inter densas, umbrosa cacumina, fagos
adsidue veniebat. ibi haec incondita solus
5 montibus et silvis studio iactabat inani:
'o crudelis Alexi, nihil mea carmina curas?
nil nostri miserere? mori me denique coges?
nunc etiam pecudes umbras et frigora captant;
nunc viridis etiam occultant spineta lacertos,
10 Thestylis[2] et rapido fessis messoribus aestu
alia serpyllumque[3] herbas contundit olentis.
at mecum raucis, tua dum vestigia lustro,
sole sub ardenti resonant arbusta cicadis.
nonne fuit satius tristis Amaryllidis iras
15 atque superba pati fastidia, nonne Menalcan[4],
quamvis ille niger, quamvis tu candidus esses?
o formose puer, nimium ne crede colori!
alba ligustra[5] cadunt, vaccinia[6] nigra leguntur.

---

[1]Corydon是一位牧人，爱上了Alexis，但后者是一位奴隶。他们两位与Alexis的奴隶主都是男性。

[2]Thestylis是一个女子的名字。

[3]serpyllum指Thymus serpyllum，野百里香或叫铺地百里香。

[4]Menalcas是一位男性。

[5]ligustrum指女贞属植物，开一串串的白花。

[6]vaccinium原指Vaccinium myrtillus，黑果越橘，又叫欧洲蓝莓或者山桑子，果实是接近全黑的蓝色。在这里更可能是代指女贞的果实，也是类似的黑色小浆果。

牧歌·其二

牧人Corydon热恋上了美丽的Alexis，
但那也是主人的宠娃——
心之所愿，宛若梦中之花；
他时时来这榉树繁密的阴影下，
向着高山说起胡编的情话，
朝着空林吐诉无谓的挣扎：
"啊，Alexis，你心若磐石！
你似从未关心我的歌词？
你也从未共情我的相思？
最后竟要将我活活逼死？
现在连牛羊也要寻找树荫和清凉，
现在连绿蜥也要钻进荆棘丛躲藏，
收割麦田的人们疲于这滚滚热浪，
Thestylis正在捣碎大蒜和野百里香[1]。
我却顶着那似火的烈日骄阳，
独自循着你的足迹来回游荡，
林间传来夏蝉那空洞的回响。
是不是该去忍受忧郁的Amaryllis，
她那娇气和傲气？
或是Menalcas，即使他黝黑如夜——
但是你的皮肤白皙似雪！
噢，美貌的少年，不要太相信肤色！
洁白的女贞花黯然凋谢，
亮黑的小浆果供人采撷！

---

[1]这可能是一种叫moretum的菜。

despectus tibi sum, nec qui sim quaeris, Alexi,

20 quam dives pecoris, nivei quam lactis abundans.

mille meae Siculis[1] errant in montibus agnae;

lac mihi non aestate novum, non frigore defit.

canto quae solitus, si quando armenta vocabat,

Amphion[2] Dircaeus in Actaeo[3] Aracyntho[4].

25 nec sum adeo informis: nuper me in litore vidi,

cum placidum ventis staret mare; non ego Daphnim[5]

iudice te metuam, si numquam fallit imago.

o tantum libeat mecum tibi sordida rura

atque humilis habitare casas, et figere cervos,

30 haedorumque gregem viridi compellere hibisco[6]!

mecum una in silvis imitabere Pana[7] canendo.

Pan primus calamos cera coniungere pluris

instituit; Pan curat ovis oviumque magistros.

---

[1] Siculi即Sicilia岛（今Sicily岛）上的居民。

[2] 神话传说里有多位Amphion，按照上下文的描述，这里最有可能的应该是神王Zeus（即Juppiter）与Antiope生下的双胞胎兄弟Amphion与Zethus。而Dirce是Antiope的叔母或者伯母，曾养育并虐待两兄弟，后被他们杀死。这些人都属于古希腊城邦Thebes的王族。Amphion的情人，商业与旅者之神Hermes（即Mercury）教会他唱歌，并赠与他lyre诗琴。传说中他的歌声里有魔法，能移动石头，也以此建造了Thebes的Cadmea堡的城墙。

[3] 指Attica半岛，位于希腊中部，著名的Athens就在此处。

[4] Aracynthus是Attica地区与Boeotia地区交界地的一座山脉。Thebes就位于Boeotia地区。Amphion兄弟早年曾在附近的Cithaeron山上当牧人。

[5] Daphnis可能是Mercury之子（一说是情人），在Sicily岛上牧羊，传说是放牧诗歌的先驱，也是一位美男子。Pan神也曾钟情于他，教他吹奏Pan笛。

[6] hibiscum指Althaea officinalis，中文名为药葵或者药蜀葵，是一种草本的药用植物，也是炼金术原料。它的根可以做成药用的甜食，后来演化成为现今的棉花糖。marshmallow一词由此而来。它的茎秆有一到两米长，这里用来做牧人赶羊的工具，晒干后也可以用来编制篮子等器具。但是hibiscus这个词在现代被用来命名木槿属的植物，一般是灌木。

[7] Pan神，荒野与畜牧之神，人身羊角羊腿。传说他用nymph妖精Syrinx变成的芦苇制作了排箫，又称为Pan笛或者排笛。

啊，Alexis！你对我如此轻视，

甚至，你都不问我是何方人士！

我富有多少成群的牛羊，

我拥有多少雪白的乳汁！

我那数以千计的母羊，

在Sicilia的高山上游荡，

我从不缺新鲜的奶香，

无论是天热还是天凉！

我的歌声，如同Amphion，用他魔法般的喉嗓，

在Aracynthus的山上，召唤他的牛羊！

我可真没那么狰狞！

最近趁着海上风平浪静，

我刚刚看了自己的倒影；

要不你来做个裁判，

如果大海没有欺瞒，

跟Daphnis[1]比，我可不会忌惮！

噢，真盼着你来跟我同住，

简陋的乡下，小小的草屋，

我们一起去狩猎公鹿，

拿着翠绿的药葵挥舞，

带着成群的羊羔散步！

随我一道，在林中模仿Pan神的歌谣——

是那Pan神最早，用蜡制作多管排箫，

是那Pan神将牧人关照，连同那些羊羔！

---

[1]也有可能这里Daphnis只是村里的另外一位男子（参见III.12）；又或者这个村里的Daphnis就是神话传说中的Daphanis，那这些村民就是在Sicily岛上放牧。

nec te paeniteat calamo trivisse labellum:

35   haec eadem ut sciret, quid non faciebat Amyntas[1]?

est mihi disparibus septem compacta cicutis[2]

fistula, Damoetas[3] dono mihi quam dedit olim,

et dixit moriens: 'te nunc habet ista secundum.'

dixit Damoetas, invidit stultus Amyntas.

40   praeterea duo, nec tuta mihi valle reperti,

capreoli[4], sparsis etiam nunc pellibus albo,

bina die siccant ovis ubera; quos tibi servo.

iam pridem a me illos abducere Thestylis orat;

et faciet, quoniam sordent tibi munera nostra.

45   huc ades, o formose puer: tibi lilia plenis

ecce ferunt nymphae[5] calathis; tibi candida Nais[6],

pallentis violas[7] et summa papavera carpens,

narcissum et florem iungit bene olentis anethi[8];

---

[1]Amyntas是一位男性的名字。

[2]cituta指Cicuta virosa毒芹，或者是Conium maculatum毒参，一种有毒植物。英文名为hemlock，这里大概是用其茎秆做芦管，或者是指代用来做排箫管的植物茎。

[3]Damoetas是另一位男性的名字。

[4]capreolus可能是一种野山羊，或者羚羊，或者西方狍（一种鹿），按照后文白色斑纹推断，更可能是狍。

[5]nympha即nymph女神或称nymph妖精，是一大类低阶女神的统称。

[6]Nais指一种水之妖精，是nymph妖精中的一类。

[7]viola是一种堇菜，多为紫色或者黄色，最常见的如Viola odorata香堇，不是现代命名的紫罗兰。

[8]anethum指Anethum graveolens，中文叫莳萝，一种香料植物。一说是Pimpinella anisum，中文叫茴芹或西洋茴香，与茴香有类似的香味。两者的花穗看上去差别也不大，可能仙女们自己也不知道采的到底是哪种，更别提译者了。

你的嘴唇会被芦管磨破，

但是不要因此畏畏缩缩，

为了学会这事，Amyntas有什么不愿做？

我这儿有把七管的长短排箫，

是Damoetas给我的礼物，

之前他临死时将其托付：

'现今它有你做第二任物主。'

他只是这样说，

那愚蠢的Amyntas就一直嫉妒！

在那险峻的山谷，

我还找到过两只小鹿，

至今皮毛上，白色的斑纹遍布，

每天要两次喝光我的羊乳！

这俩那Thestylis一直跟我央求，

我却一直为你预留；

既然我的礼物令你蒙羞，

那就让她带走！

美丽的少年，快来吧，看！

为你，nymph仙女们，

带来了满满一篮的百合花，

为你，亮白的水之妖精，

把淡雅的香堇和最美的罂粟摘下，

把水仙花与香味浓郁的莳萝混搭；

tum casia[1] atque aliis intexens suavibus herbis,

50 mollia luteola pingit vaccinia[2] calta[3].

ipse ego cana legam tenera lanugine mala[4],

castaneasque nuces, mea quas Amaryllis amabat;

addam cerea pruna: honos erit huic quoque pomo;

et vos, o lauri[5], carpam, et te, proxima myrte[6],

55 sic positae quoniam suavis miscetis odores.

rusticus es, Corydon, nec munera curat Alexis,

nec, si muneribus certes, concedat Iollas[7].

heu, heu, quid volui misero mihi! floribus Austrum[8]

perditus et liquidis inmisi fontibus apros.

60 quem fugis, ah, demens? habitarunt di quoque silvas,

Dardaniusque[9] Paris[10]. Pallas[11], quas condidit arces,

ipsa colat; nobis placeant ante omnia silvae.

---

[1] casia可以指Laurus cassia，野肉桂，一种类似肉桂的树，或者是Daphne mezereum，欧洲的瑞香花，是一种重要的蜜源植物。参见《农事诗》II.213,466。这里动词intexo如果理解成编织，则更有可能是瑞香，如果理解成在周围铺上，则更可能是野肉桂。

[2] 参见前注II.18。

[3] calta又作caltha，大概是Calendula officinalis，金盏花，又叫金盏菊，有艳黄色或者橘黄色的花。

[4] malum可能是各种的水果，比如苹果，榅桲，桃子，橙子，石榴等等。这里按照软毛白果的描述，可能是桃子，也可能是榅桲。

[5] laurus即Laurus nobilis，月桂，是代表Apollo的圣树。

[6] myrtum即Myrtus communis，香桃木，又称桃金娘，是爱神Aphrodite（即Venus）的圣花。

[7] Iollas是一个男性的名字，这里看可能是前文中Alexis的男主人，也可能是另外一位Alexis的追求者。

[8] Auster，南风之神。

[9] Dardanus这里指代Troia，即古城Troy。

[10] Paris即Troia的王子，由于他掳走了美女Helen，引发了Troia战争。还是婴儿时，他在附近的Ida山上独自存活了九天；而他早年也作为牧民，住在山野之地。

[11] Pallas是智慧女神Athena即Minerva的别名。

她把野肉桂连同其他的香味杂草铺撒，

她用软软的山桑和黄色的金盏菊作画！

我会亲自挑选那带软毛的白桃，

还有那栗子，曾是我的Amaryllis[1]的喜好；

还有那蜡一般的李子——

给这果实也带来荣耀！

还有你，月桂，我要采摘你的模样，

加上你，触手可及的桃金娘，

这样你们能混合出那迷人的芳香！

啊，Corydon，你只是个乡巴佬！

Alexis也不屑你的礼包，

再说，若是只拿礼物比较，

那你怎可能比Iollas的更好！

哎哟，哎哟！

不知道在想啥呢，可怜的我！

迷茫的我！

让南风之神摧残花朵！

让野猪在清泉里撒泼！

啊，你[2]在逃避谁呢？你这傻瓜！

算上那Paris，他来自Troia，

还有神明们也都在林中安家，

就让Athena住在她自己建的高塔[3]，

这林子比什么都让人解乏。

---

[1] 从这里与II.14推断，Amaryllis大概是Corydon的妻子。夫妻二人有可能是Tityrus赎身时的主人。

[2] 这里"你"还是自指。

[3] 原文是堡垒或者城堡。但是查不到Athena有自己建房子的记录，一说指Athens。

torva leaena lupum sequitur; lupus ipse capellam;

florentem cytisum[1] sequitur lasciva capella;

65   te Corydon, o Alexi: trahit sua quemque voluptas.

aspice, aratra iugo referunt suspensa iuvenci,

et sol crescentis decedens duplicat umbras:

me tamen urit amor; quis enim modus adsit amori?

ah, Corydon, Corydon, quae te dementia cepit!

70   semiputata tibi frondosa vitis in ulmo est;

quin tu aliquid saltem potius, quorum indiget usus,

viminibus mollique paras detexere iunco?

invenies alium, si te hic fastidit, Alexim.'

---

[1] 参见I.79注。

凶残的母狮追逐着狼，

狼自己追逐着山羊，

欢闹的羊追逐着苜蓿的花香；

Corydon也追逐着你，Alexis，

每个人都追逐着自己的欲望[1]！

你看！

共轭的公牛带着铁犁[2]回家，

渐长的阴影随着夕阳落下；

可我还是被这爱意裹挟[3]，

这爱意哪里有什么边界！

Corydon啊，Corydon！

你被什么抓住了心弦！

在榆树上[4]，你还有一半的葡萄枝叶没有修剪；

至少你更该准备去编些实用的物件，

拿柔枝和软软的灯心草打发下时间？

若是这个Alexis不喜欢你，

你，总能找到另一个代替。"

---

[1]原文是"自己的欲望拉扯着每个人"。

[2]原文是带着"悬犁"，即耕完地不用的时候把犁头悬空，拖曳着回家，防止其磨损。可能是将整个犁反转过来，也可能是在下面垫上了木制的轮毂结构。

[3]原文是"燃烧"。

[4]葡萄经常被挂在榆树上。这里的榆树相当于现代的葡萄棚。

ECLOGA III

起于一只母羊的口水仗，牧人Damoetas
和Menalcas开始互相揶揄，继而相约赛歌决
定胜负，把村里的大大小小的情事都抖了出
来。

ECLOGA III

M. Dic mihi, Damoeta[1], cuium pecus, an Meliboei?

D. non, verum Aegonis; nuper mihi tradidit Aegon[2].

M. infelix o semper, ovis, pecus, ipse Neaeram[3]
dum fovet, ac ne me sibi praeferat illa veretur,
5   hic alienus ovis custos bis mulget in hora,
et sucus pecori et lac subducitur agnis.

D. parcius ista viris tamen obicienda memento:
novimus et qui te, transversa tuentibus hircis[4],
et quo—sed faciles nymphae[5] risere—sacello.

10 **M.** tum, credo, cum me arbustum videre Miconis[6]
atque mala vitis incidere falce novellas.

---

[1]这里开始是两位牧人Damoetas与Menalcas的对话。
[2]Aegon是一位男性的名字。
[3]Neaera是一位女性的名字。
[4]公羊面前，也可能暗示是跟母羊。
[5]见前注II.46。
[6]Micon是一位男性的名字。

牧歌·其三

M. 告诉我，Damoetas，
这是谁的羊，或是Meliboeus？

D. 不是，是Aegon的羊，
Aegon刚刚托我喂养。

M. 噢，羊儿啊，你总是那么不幸！
那主人自己，跑去找Neaera保持感情，
总是怕她更喜欢我，真是他的心病！
他找个不认识[1]的监护，
每个小时[2]挤两次羊乳，
甜汁从乳房全部流出，
让那羊羔饿坏了肚肚！

D. 记得嚼舌根的时候也得心虚——
我可知是谁和你小聚，
在公羊注视之下欢愉，
在哪座神庙之中云雨；
好脾气的nymph仙女，
怕只是当作闲趣！

M. 我想，那时在Micon的果园，
她们也看到是我，
用那恶毒的镰刀，
砍断新栽的葡萄？

---

[1]这里只是讽刺Damoetas像陌生人一样对待Aegon的羊。
[2]从日出到日落划分为十二个小时，约等于现行的小时。

D.   aut hic ad veteres fagos cum Daphnidis[1] arcum
      fregisti et calamos: quae tu, perverse[2] Menalca,
      et cum vidisti puero donata, dolebas,
15   et si non aliqua nocuisses, mortuus esses.

M.   quid domini faciant, audent cum talia fures!
      non ego te vidi Damonis[3], pessime, caprum
      excipere insidiis, multum latrante Lycisca[4]?
      et cum clamarem: 'quo nunc se proripit ille?
20   Tityre[5], coge pecus,' tu post carecta latebas.

D.   an mihi cantando victus non redderet ille
      quem mea carminibus meruisset fistula caprum?
      si nescis, meus ille caper fuit; et mihi Damon
      ipse fatebatur, sed reddere posse negabat.

---

[1]Daphnis，参见II.26注。II里他是美男子，这里还是小男孩。

[2]preversus也可以指Manalcas跟Daphnis赛歌落败，然后气急之下把比赛押注的弓箭弄坏。

[3]Damon是一位男性的名字。

[4]Lycisca应该是条狗。按上下文看是Damon或是Tityrus的狗。

[5]很有可能这时候Tityrus还是Damon的奴隶，如果是这样的话Damon就是I.31里Galatea的丈夫，也是Tityrus的前任主人。而Amaryllis和Corydon也可能是他们的女儿女婿，或是妹妹妹夫。

D. 或是在这古老的榉树华盖，

你把Daphnis的弓与箭折歪；

你，Menalcas，心眼真是坏，

见到收礼物的男孩，

你的心里就不痛快，

不找点法子把他害，

你，就成天想不开[1]！

M. 小偷都如此胆大包天，

那主人家该如何应变？

我难道没有看见，

那个谁，最下贱！

用诡计去抓Damon的羊，

那Lycisca叫得汪汪！

而当我高声呼喊：

"那家伙现在跑去哪撒欢？

Tityrus，快来把羊聚团！"

你那时就躲在草丛后的阴暗！

D. 这羊可是我的芦管[2]斗歌应得之赏，

输了比赛的他难道不该双手奉上？

所以你是有所不知，这曾是我的羊，

连Damon他自己也是承认这般，

只是他，拒绝归还[3]！

---

　　[1]原文是"就像已经死了"。

　　[2]参见II.37。II里Damoetas已经去世。而从他死时将排箫赠与Corydon得知，他与Damon家应该是亲戚朋友之类的良好关系。同理前面也大多是戏谑之词，比如老顽童弄坏了儿童的玩具，帮工不小心弄折了葡萄藤。

　　[3]可能是他妻子Galatea不肯承认赌约，参见I.31。

25 **M.**   cantando tu illum? aut umquam tibi fistula cera
   iuncta fuit? non tu in triviis, indocte, solebas
   stridenti miserum stipula disperdere carmen?

 D. vis ergo inter nos quid possit uterque vicissim
   experiamur? ego hanc vitulam—ne forte recuses,
30   bis venit ad mulctram, binos alit ubere fetus—
   depono: tu dic, mecum quo pignore certes.

 M. de grege non ausim quicquam deponere tecum.
   est mihi namque domi pater, est iniusta noverca;
   bisque die numerant ambo pecus, alter et haedos.
35   verum, id quod multo tute ipse fatebere maius,
   insanire libet quoniam tibi, pocula ponam
   fagina, caelatum divini opus Alcimedontis[1];

---

[1]Alcimedon大概是一位木雕的工匠。 按照后文，两个人都随身拿出他做
的杯子，说明很可能只是当地木匠，而那些赞美之词也只是浮夸。

M. 你的歌声居然比他还妙？
　　　你何时曾有蜡粘的排箫？
　　　难道不是你，没有老师教，
　　　难道不是你，在那三叉道，
　　　总是拿陋管的尖啸，
　　　滥奏那不幸的歌谣？

D. 那要不我们来比试一番，
　　　轮流把本事让对方看看。
　　　我，押上这只小母牛——
　　　你别小瞧，她挤两次奶[1]，
　　　还要喂饱，两只小牛崽——
　　　你说说，你拿什么押注，跟我比赛？

M. 可不敢拿什么牲畜跟你下注。
　　　我家中还有老父，
　　　还有刻薄的继母[2]！
　　　两个人每天两次清点羊群的数目，
　　　他们还轮流着，连那羊羔都要数！
　　　既然你只是脑子进水，
　　　我就押上这榉木酒杯[3]，
　　　你自己也得承认，这比牛更贵——
　　　可以与天神的媲美，
　　　Alcimedon的光辉！

---

[1]应该是每天挤两次奶的意思。但是万一赌输了，可以说"我可没说是每天两次"。
[2]参见《农事诗》II.128,III.282。
[3]原文没有说数量，但是是复数，很可能是一对。

lenta quibus torno[1] facili superaddita vitis

diffusos hedera[2] vestit pallente corymbos:

40   in medio duo signa, Conon[3], et—quis fuit alter,

descripsit radio totum qui gentibus orbem,

tempora quae messor, quae curvus arator haberet?

necdum illis labra admovi, sed condita servo.

D.   et nobis idem Alcimedon duo pocula fecit,

45   et molli circum est ansas amplexus acantho[4],

Orpheaque[5] in medio posuit silvasque sequentis.

necdum illis labra admovi, sed condita servo.

si ad vitulam spectas, nihil est quod pocula laudes.

M.   nunquam hodie effugies; veniam, quocumque vocaris.

50   audiat haec tantum—vel qui venit ecce Palaemon[6].

efficiam posthac ne quemquam voce lacessas.

---

[1] tornus是木工活使用的打磨轮（参见《农事诗》II.449），基本上不可能用来磨出文中描述的细节。这里只是夸张或者反讽的说法。

[2] hedera指Hedera helix，常春藤，有蓝黑色成簇的小果实。

[3] Conon是古希腊天文学家和数学家，出生在Samos岛上，后来成为埃及的宫廷学者，是著名的Archimedes的朋友。而文中另一位很可能是同时期的学者，首次丈量地球周长的Eratosthenes，也可能是Archimedes或其他做了类似工作的学者。

[4] acanthus指茛苕，常用于建筑浮雕装饰。但是要能在杯子把手上雕出它，那的确是鬼斧神工。

[5] Orpheus是希腊神话中的人物，擅长音乐，传说歌声能让树木移动。曾下冥府试图拯救他的妻子Eurydice。参见《农事诗》IV.453-527。

[6] Palaemon是位男性，是参与对话的第三人。

这柔软的葡萄藤欣欣向荣，
便是拿方便的打磨轮加工！
又点缀上那苍白的常春藤，
上面串串的果实密集茂盛！
图案的中央，有两个雕像：
一位是Conon，另一位是那谁？
为全体人类他用木杖，
把整个地球拿来测量；
指导人们何时收割，
何时弯腰下地耕作。
我的嘴唇没有碰过，
就跟全新的差不多[1]！

D.　同样这个Alcimedon也给我做了两个酒杯，
　　这杯柄周围有柔软的莨苕[2]；
　　中间画着Orpheus，还有树木跟着他跑！
　　我的嘴唇从没碰到，
　　就跟全新的一样好[3]！
　　但这小母牛你只要一瞧，
　　那这杯子就不值得夸耀！

M.　你今天可别想逃！
　　你无论押什么，我都跟到！
　　只是要找个人来比较——
　　看！有人来了，是Palaemon！
　　我可保证，让你今后不敢再找人比赛歌谣！

---

[1] 原文是一直保存得很好的意思。
[2] 莨音艮，苕音勺或条。
[3] 这里47行与上文43行原文一模一样。

D. quin age, si quid habes, in me mora non erit ulla,
nec quemquam fugio: tantum, vicine Palaemon,
sensibus haec imis, res est non parva, reponas.

55 **P.** dicite, quandoquidem in molli consedimus herba.
et nunc omnis ager, nunc omnis parturit arbos,
nunc frondent silvae, nunc formosissimus annus.
incipe, Damoeta; tu deinde sequere, Menalca:
alternis dicetis; amant alterna Camenae[1].

60 **D.** ab Iove[2] principium, Musae[3]; Iovis omnia plena:
ille colit terras, illi mea carmina curae.

M. et me Phoebus[4] amat; Phoebo sua semper apud me
munera sunt, lauri et suave rubens hyacinthus[5].

---

[1]Camenae原指罗马神话中司职泉水和生育的女神。她们很可能属于nymph一类，有四位，而其中只有Carmenta有诗歌的属性，而另外两位Antevorta和Postvorta司职未来与过去，也被认为是Carmenta的两面。而也有人将她们混同于Muse女神（最普遍认为是九位），所以这里也可能只是指代Muse。

[2]即第三代神王Juppiter，对应希腊神话中的*Zeus*，是Muse女神们的父亲。

[3]一说这里Muse也是指代诗歌，即"从Juppiter开始我的歌谣"之意。

[4]Phoebus意为光明，一般作为*Apollo*的别名。参见II.54注。

[5]Hyacinthus原是*Apollo*眷恋的美少年。但这里hyacinthus不是现代命名的风信子（原产亚洲，直到十六世纪才引进欧洲），而是Gladiolus communis唐菖蒲，参见《农事诗》IV.137。

D. 不管你有什么，来比!
　　我不会有任何迟疑，
　　我也不会选择逃避!
　　Palaemon啊，临街的你，
　　你可得用点心，这可不是儿戏!

P. 既然我们已经坐上这柔软的草地，
　　你们就开始唱起!
　　如今所有的田地都丰收在望，
　　如今所有的树木都硕果飘香，
　　如今所有的森林都绿叶茫茫，
　　如今真是一年中最美的模样!
　　Damoetas，你先来，
　　Menalcas，你等待!
　　你们轮流唱开，
　　对唱的歌，Carmenta女神[1]最爱!

D. Muse女神，你们最初，
　　来自Juppiter，伟大的天父!
　　他滋润了万物，
　　他开垦了田土，
　　他聆听我的音符!

M. Phoebus一直对我眷顾!
　　我也一直随身带着给他的礼物:
　　神圣的月桂叶，柔红的唐菖蒲!

---

[1] 参见前页注。

D. malo me Galatea[1] petit, lasciva[2] puella,
　　　et fugit ad salices, et se cupit ante videri.

65

M. at mihi sese offert ultro, meus ignis, Amyntas,
　　　notior ut iam sit canibus non Delia[3] nostris.

D. parta meae Veneri[4] sunt munera: namque notavi
　　　ipse locum, aeriae quo congessere palumbes.

70 **M.** quod potui, puero silvestri ex arbore lecta
　　　aurea mala decem misi; cras altera mittam.

D. o quotiens et quae nobis Galatea locuta est!
　　　partem aliquam, venti, divum referatis ad auris!

M. quid prodest, quod me ipse animo non spernis, Amynta.
75　　si, dum tu sectaris apros, ego retia servo?

---

[1]这里斗歌一唱一和不一定说真实的或者自己的事情，而且可能按照前文体例，部分有可能是互相揶揄对方的事情。比如Amyntas喜欢Damoetas（参见II.35,39）；而这里Galatea还是个小姑娘，喜欢Menalcas。这些很可能都是他们的陈年往事。

[2]这个词也可以形容活泼的或者好动的，但是按照上下文应该还是淫荡好色的意思。

[3]Delia是*Artemis*（Diana）的别名，很可能源自*Apollo*与*Artemis*出生的的Delos岛。这里大概指代月亮或者月光。也有认为这里只是一个女仆的名字。

[4]Venus，爱神，这里大概指代爱人。

D. Galatea那小姑娘真淫贱，
给的苹果真是甜，
她逃进了柳林间，
还盼着我能看见!

M. Amyntas啊，我的欲火!
他自己会投怀送抱给我!
我家的狗狗见他的次数，
比那轮明月还要多得多[1]!

D. 我寻到礼物，给我的爱恋，
我已在那里标记地点，
高处林鸽[2]的爱巢之间。

M. 我能做的都已经做:
给那男孩[3]十个金果，
从那野树林中寻获，
明日的我要给更多!

D. 噢，Galatea曾对我有多少媚语!
风啊，请带一些去给神明!

M. Amyntas，你去追猎野猪，
我在看守猎网，
你把我放心上，
但是又能怎样?

---

[1]这段有很强的调侃语气，应该是揶揄对方的事情。
[2]就是I.57里Tityrus最爱的林鸽。所以Menalcas有可能喜欢Tityrus?
[3]可能指Amyntas。

D. Phyllida[1] mitte mihi: meus est natalis, Iolla;
cum faciam vitula pro frugibus, ipse venito.

M. Phyllida amo ante alias; nam me discedere flevit,
et longum 'formose, vale, vale,' inquit, Iolla[2].

80 **D.** triste lupus stabulis, maturis frugibus imbres.
arboribus venti, nobis Amaryllidis irae.

M. dulce satis umor, depulsis arbutus haedis,
lenta salix feto pecori, mihi solus Amyntas.

D. Pollio[3] amat nostram, quamvis est rustica, Musam[4]:
85 Pierides[5], vitulam lectori pascite vestro.

M. Pollio et ipse facit nova carmina: pascite taurum,
iam cornu petat et pedibus qui spargat arenam.

---

[1]Phyllis是一位女性，从文中看大概是Iollas的女儿或者女奴隶。

[2]这里标点也可以将Iolla 标入引号内，视为Phyllis说的话的一部分。那么这里一唱一和就成了模仿村里某人和Iollas的对话。但是这样的话"我离开时她泪汪汪"似乎就说不通。

[3]Pollio可能只是一位男性的村民，更可能是Gaius Asinius Pollio或者是代表他形象的虚拟人物。他本人是古罗马的军人，政客和诗人，作者的朋友。

[4]这里的Muse应该同I.2里指代诗歌。

[5]Pierides又称为Emathides，是神话中与Muse斗歌的九姐妹。有的时候Muse也被混称为Pierides。这里很可能指村里喜欢唱歌的几个村姑，就像是中文语境"村口的西施"。让Muse女神去给Pollio喂牛似乎于理不通，存疑。

D. Iollas，务必让Phyllis过来，当帮手[1]，
今天是我要做寿；
当我献祭小母牛，为丰收，
你也过来瞅一瞅！

M. Iollas，我爱Phyllis胜于其他的姑娘[2]，
我离开时她两眼汪汪，
"再见，再见，美少年"在风中回荡！

D. 恶狼之于羊圈的悲伤，
豪雨之于成熟的果香，
暴风之于参天的树林，
Amaryllis的怒火之于我身。

M. 湿气之于谷物的甜蜜，
野莓之于断奶的羊羔，
柔枝之于怀孕的兽群，
唯有Amyntas之于我心。

D. Pollio喜欢我们的歌谣，尽管那很乡土，
"Muse[3]"们啊，快去给你们的读者[4]喂牛犊！

M. Pollio自己也创作新稿，
你们[5]也得把公牛喂饱，
它有会伤人的犄角，
它把沙尘踢得高高。

---

[1] 也有将Phyllis送给或者嫁给自己的意思。
[2] 这里alias指其他女性。暗示Damoetas可能更喜欢男性。
[3] 见前页注。
[4] 读者是指Pollio，见下文，说他也能写作。
[5] 指前文的"Muse"。

D. qui te, Pollio, amat, veniat quo te quoque gaudet:
mella fluant illi, ferat et rubus asper amomum[1].

90 **M.** qui Bavium[2] non odit, amet tua carmina, Maevi,
atque idem iungat vulpes et mulgeat hircos.

D. qui legitis flores et humi nascentia fraga,
frigidus, o pueri, fugite hinc, latet anguis in herba.

M. parcite, oves, nimium procedere; non bene ripae
95 creditur; ipse aries etiam nunc vellera siccat.

D. Tityre, pascentes a flumine reice capellas:
ipse ubi tempus erit, omnis in fonte lavabo.

M. cogite ovis, pueri; si lac praeceperit aestus,
ut nuper, frustra pressabimus ubera palmis.

100 **D.** heu, heu, quam pingui macer est mihi taurus in ervo[3]!

---

[1]amomum是一种芳香植物，可以制作香膏；可能是Cissus vitiginea蔓白粉藤。

[2]Bavius与Maevius似乎是作者同时期的诗人，没有作品留世。

[3]ervum可能是Vicia ervilia，一种苦味的野豌豆，或者其他类似的豆类。

D. 谁若是喜欢[1]Pollio 你，
　　就让他来这，你欢喜之地；
　　为了他，无用的荆棘，
　　散发了芳香，流出了甜蜜！

M. 谁若是不讨厌Bavius，
　　就让他喜欢你的歌，Maevius；
　　也让他给狐狸上轭耕地，
　　再去把公羊的奶头挤挤！

D. 啊，孩子们！
　　你们在地上摘鲜花，在草中寻草莓——
　　快跑，那草里藏着蛇，冰冷似水！

M. 啊，羊儿们！
　　不要走太远，不要太相信河岸，
　　公羊现在还在那儿把羊毛晾干！

D. Tityrus啊，
　　把吃草的母山羊从河边赶回，
　　我到时会带它们去泡泡泉水。

M. 孩子们，把母羊召回，
　　若像上次，暑气带走了奶水，
　　挤奶的手力可是白费！

D. 哎，豆子如此肥沃，
　　哎，公牛如此瘦弱！

---

[1]这里的喜欢是喜欢Pollio的作品的意思，见下文Bavius与Maevius。

idem amor exitium pecori pecorisque magistro[1].

M. his certe neque amor causa est; vix ossibus haerent.
nescio quis teneros oculus mihi fascinat agnos.

D. dic, quibus in terris—et eris mihi magnus Apollo—
105   tris pateat caeli spatium non amplius ulnas[2].

M. dic, quibus in terris inscripti nomina regum
nascantur flores, et Phyllida solus habeto.

P. non nostrum inter vos tantas componere lites.
et vitula tu dignus, et hic, et quisquis amores
110   aut metuet dulces, aut experietur amaros.
claudite iam rivos, pueri, sat prata biberunt.

---

[1]这里magister不一定是牲畜的主人，而仅仅是牧羊人。
[2]ulna指前臂，这里用做长度单位。

　　同样的爱欲之火，
　　燃尽了牲畜[1]，
　　燃尽了放牧的小伙！

M. 它们饿得皮包骨头，
　　肯定不是为爱发愁，
　　不知是那谁的眼球，
　　盯上了肥美的羊肉。

D. 你要是能想起，
　　是在哪块土地，
　　苍穹最高超不过三臂？
　　你于我，就是伟大的Apollo！

M. 你要是能说清，
　　是在哪块秘境，
　　花朵都标着国王之名[2]？
　　你这厮，就独自占有Phyllis！

P. 我可没法给你们分出胜者。
　　那只母牛，你和他都该得；
　　还有无论是谁，
　　管他是惧怕过爱的欢乐，
　　或者是经历过爱的苦涩！
　　孩子们呐，
　　停下你们的口若悬河，
　　这草地已经宛若泽国！

---

[1] 公牛的爱情故事，参见《农事诗》III.220-241。
[2] 这两个谜语，答案可能是蜂巢。

ECLOGA IV

　　朋友家生了一个小孩，诗人用泛滥华丽的辞藻给小孩的出生写了祝词，最后只是让小宝宝多笑笑。

ECLOGA IV

Sicelides Musae[1], paulo maiora canamus!
non omnis arbusta iuvant humilesque myricae;
si canimus silvas, silvae sint consule dignae.

ultima Cumaei[2] venit iam carminis aetas;
5   magnus ab integro saeclorum nascitur ordo:
iam redit et Virgo[3], redeunt Saturnia[4] regna;
iam nova progenies caelo demittitur alto.

tu modo nascenti puero, quo ferrea primum
desinet ac toto surget gens aurea mundo,
10   casta fave Lucina[5]: tuus iam regnat Apollo.

teque adeo decus hoc aevi, te consule[6], inibit,
Pollio, et incipient magni procedere menses.

te duce, si qua manent sceleris vestigia nostri,
inrita perpetua solvent formidine terras.

---

[1]Sicilia的Muse，这里也可能是致敬在Sicily岛上的Syracuse出生的诗人Theocritus，田园牧歌的创始人。本书大多数人名来自Theocritus的田园诗*Idylls*。Muse似乎没有在Sicilia岛上活动的记录，可能是指代文中的几个女孩。

[2]Cumae在Campania，是希腊人在Italia的第一个殖民地。有*Apollo*的神庙和女祭司，以预言闻名。Cumae之歌大概是泛指某个预言。

[3]这里很可能指公平女神Astraea，即处女座，白银时代最后一位离开人间的神祇。

[4]Saturnus，即第二代神王*Cronus*，在他的治下，人们无需工作，农田自己长出果实，河流里流淌着葡萄酒，生活富足轻松。

[5]Lucina是罗马神话中掌管生育的女神（或者是职位）。一说是Juno即天后*Hera*，一说是Diana即*Artemis*，这里应该指后者，即*Apollo*的妹妹。

[6]作者的朋友Pollio在前40年担任执政。但是11-14行这段话跟孩子没有任何关系。似乎文本有过改动。也可能只是说，现今执政治下，天下太平，小孩子能享受快乐的人生。

牧歌·其四

Sicilia的Muse啊，

让我们稍稍唱起更加宏伟的歌声！

果园和低微的柳柽[1]，

不能满足各色人等；

若是歌唱那片丛林，

也要让它媲美执政！

Cumae之歌中的终极纪元已经到来，

崭新的伟大秩序诞生在我们的时代！

如今处女神Astraea正重回地面，

Saturnus的统治也正重返人间！

如今一位全新的神裔，

从那高高的天宇降临！

圣洁的Lucina啊，请庇佑那新生的男孩[2]，

他要首先终结黑铁的时代，

在大地上开启黄金的纪元：

如今你的Apollo，君临四海！

你，Pollio啊，当你为执政，

时间将进入这荣光的永恒，

这伟大的年岁将开启征程！

由你的领导，

让我们残存的罪恶足迹云散烟消，

让大地脱离这片无边恐惧的笼罩！

---

[1] 柽音撑，myrica柽柳是一种低矮的灌木。

[2] 这个男孩是谁众说纷纭。这里有可能只是村里新生的孩子，而全篇那些滥用的赞美只是类似"你家公子气宇不凡，如文曲星君下凡"之类的捧场之词。

15 ille deum vitam accipiet divisque videbit

permixtos heroas et ipse videbitur illis,

pacatumque reget patriis virtutibus orbem.

at tibi prima, puer, nullo munuscula cultu

errantis hederas passim cum baccare[1] tellus

20 mixtaque ridenti colocasia[2] fundet acantho[3].

ipsae lacte domum referent distenta capellae

ubera, nec magnos metuent armenta leones;

ipsa tibi blandos fundent cunabula flores.

occidet et serpens, et fallax herba veneni

25 occidet, Assyrium[4] volgo nascetur amomum[5].

at simul heroum laudes et facta parentis

iam legere et quae sit poteris cognoscere virtus,

molli paulatim flavescet campus arista

incultisque rubens pendebit sentibus uva

30 et durae quercus sudabunt roscida mella.

pauca tamen suberunt priscae vestigia fraudis,

quae temptare Thetim[6] ratibus, quae cingere muris

oppida, quae iubeant telluri infindere sulcos.

---

[1]baccar是哪种植物尚不明确。可能是一种香料植物，比如Valeriana Celtica，缬草，或者是cyclamen仙客来。

[2]colocasia可能指Arum colocasia，疆南星，样子有点像芋头；也有说是一种埃及豆。

[3]莨苕，参见III.45。

[4]Assyria是位于东方的一个古国，主要领土位于今Iraq和Syria等地。

[5]见III.89注。

[6]Thetis是英雄Achilles的母亲，是一位水之妖精nymph。这里很可能指代大海。

那孩子将过得像神一样富足，
眼见与诸神杂居的英雄人物；
而诸神也将对他格外关注；
他因其历代先祖的勇武，
统御这安静和平的大陆。
孩子啊，大地会自发地献出贺礼——
四散的仙客来，漫游的常青藤，
常笑的莨苕叶，遍布的疆南星。
自行归舍的山羊乳汁充盈，
牲畜也不惧怕狮子的巨大身影；
你的摇篮宛如迷人的花苑华庭！
没有毒蛇的袭扰，也没有骗人的毒草[1]，
而是遍地开花，Assyria的香料！
将来当你长大，
知晓父辈的艰难，
读懂英雄的礼赞，
了解美德的内涵，
到那时，
柔软的麦穗，会逐渐把田野染黄，
野生的荆棘，挂满了葡萄的红妆，
硬皮的橡树，甘露般的蜜汁流淌！
然而远古的罪恶仍有少量的迹象，
人们还是要乘船体验大海的激荡，
围绕小镇建起高耸的城墙，
将那垄沟刻入荒芜的草莽。

---

[1]比如和小麦很像的毒麦。

alter erit tum Tiphys, et altera quae vehat Argo[1]
35   delectos heroas; erunt etiam altera bella
atque iterum ad Troiam magnus mittetur Achilles[2].
hinc, ubi iam firmata virum te fecerit aetas,
cedet et ipse mari vector, nec nautica pinus[3]
mutabit merces: omnis feret omnia tellus;
40   non rastros patietur humus, non vinea falcem;
robustus quoque iam tauris iuga solvet arator;
nec varios discet mentiri lana colores,
ipse sed in pratis aries iam suave rubenti
murice[4], iam croceo mutabit vellera luto;
45   sponte sua sandyx[5] pascentis vestiet agnos.
'talia saecla', suis dixerunt, 'currite', fusis
concordes stabili fatorum numine Parcae[6].
adgredere o magnos—aderit iam tempus—honores,
cara deum suboles, magnum Iovis incrementum!

---

[1]Argo是古希腊英雄传说中Jason等人坐的一条船，Tiphys则是船上的舵手。

[2]Achilles是Troia战争中大放光彩的英雄人物。

[3]松木，这里指代船只。

[4]murex是一种螺类，它身上的粘液可以用作染料，即骨螺紫，又称Tyre紫，皇家紫。颜色偏红，一般作为古代最高等级的颜色，为贵族或者祭司专用。

[5]sandyx是一种红色染料，原材料大概是氧化的铅和铁，类似朱红色。

[6]Parcae是神话中的命运三女神，分别是Nona，司掌出生，将人的命运之线缠上她的纺锤（fusus）；Demica，司掌生命的长度，测量命运之线；Morta，司掌死亡，最后切断命运之线。她们可能只是生死概念的神化。

那时会有另一位Tiphys，另一艘Argo号，
满载着天选的英雄起锚；
也会有另一场战争，
伟大的Achilles会再次向Troia出征！
此后，当催人的岁月将你哺育成才，
水手不再扬帆出海，
也无需松木商船交换买卖；
所有的土地都会满足所有的期待；
土地不再需要耙子耕田，
葡萄不再需要镰刀修剪，
公牛不再需要犁轭相连，
强壮的耕夫享受着时间；
羊毛不再需要用色彩伪装：
草地上公羊，自己变幻着羊毛的模样：
一会变成迷人透红的紫妆，
一会变成藏红花[1]般的金黄，
吃草的羊羔自己穿上了朱红的衣裳！

啊，命运三姐妹，
她们紧随着永恒的神性光辉，
她们指挥着手中的司命纺锤：
"飞奔吧，这时代的壮美！"
噢，天神所爱的传人！
噢，神王的伟大子孙！
崇高的荣光向你接近，
现今这时刻即将来临！

---

[1] 藏红色，接近金黄色。

50   aspice convexo nutantem pondere mundum,

     terrasque tractusque maris caelumque profundum!

     aspice, venturo laetentur ut omnia saeclo!

     o mihi tam longae maneat pars ultima vitae,

     spiritus et quantum sat erit tua dicere facta!

55   non me carminibus vincet nec Thracius[1] Orpheus[2],

     nec Linus[3], huic mater quamvis atque huic pater adsit,

     Orphei Calliopea, Lino formosus Apollo,

     Pan[4] etiam, Arcadia[5] mecum si iudice certet,

     Pan etiam Arcadia dicat se iudice victum.

60   incipe, parve puer, risu cognoscere matrem,

     matri longa decem tulerunt fastidia menses.

     incipe, parve puer, cui non risere parenti,

     nec deus hunc mensa, dea nec dignata cubili est.

---

[1]即Thrace，古地区名，大概位置在今Bulgaria南部，Greece的东北角和Turkey的欧洲部分。

[2]参见III.46注。Orpheus的母亲是Muse女神之首的Calliope，父亲一说是*Apollo*，一说是Thrace的国王Oeagrus。

[3]Linus也是Thrace的歌手，关于他父母亲，传说的版本很多，大致认为他父亲是*Apollo*，而母亲是Muse之一的Calliope或者Urania。所以他和Orpheus有可能是同父同母或者同父异母或者同母异父的兄弟。后面这句有可能是互文，说这两兄弟都受到了父母的帮助。

[4]参见II.31。

[5]Arcadia在希腊Peloponnese半岛的中部山区。相传是Pan神的故乡。

看，这世界颤抖着支撑起苍穹之重!
这大地，这深海，这片高远的天空!
看! 万物因这即将开启的时代欢腾涌动!
噢，愿我悠长的一生，
可以延伸那最后一程，
愿我还有一息尚存，
可以歌唱你的永恒!
那来自Thrace的Orpheus或是Linus，
都无法用歌声让我服输，
即使他们还有父母襄助:
司歌的Calliope，Orpheus之母!
俊美的Apollo，Linus之父!
即使是Arcadia做裁判，
让Pan神与我比赛一番，
即使是Arcadia做裁断，
那Pan神也得自认其短!

小宝贝啊，
要开始认识你母亲的微笑，
你母亲忍受了十月的辛劳。
小宝贝啊，
要开始对父母展开笑颜，
否则就不能与天神同宴，
否则就不能与女神同眠。

ECLOGA V

牧羊人Menalcas与Mopsus在回忆Daphnis
的去世。他们还畅想了Daphnis如何进入天国
的场景，最后惺惺相惜，互赠了礼物。

ECLOGA V

Me.   Cur non, Mopse[1], boni quoniam convenimus ambo,
       tu calamos inflare levis, ego dicere versus,
       hic corylis mixtas inter consedimus ulmos?

Mo.   tu maior; tibi me est aequum parere, Menalca.
5   sive sub incertas Zephyris[2] motantibus umbras,
       sive antro potius succedimus: aspice, ut antrum
       silvestris raris sparsit labrusca[3] racemis.

Me.   montibus in nostris solus tibi certat Amyntas.

Mo.   quid, si idem certet Phoebum[4] superare canendo?

10 **Me.**   incipe, Mopse, prior, si quos aut Phyllidis ignes[5],
       aut Alconis[6] habes laudes, aut iurgia Codri.
       incipe, pascentis servabit Tityrus haedos.

Mo.   immo haec, in viridi nuper quae cortice fagi
       carmina descripsi et modulans alterna notavi,
15   experiar, tu deinde iubeto ut certet Amyntas.

---

[1]这里是两位牧人Menalcas与Mopsus的对话。

[2]Zephyr，西风之神。

[3]labrusca似乎是一种野生的葡萄。

[4]Phoebus，即*Apollo*。

[5]这里ignis可以有很多不同的意思，可能指爱火，怒火或是脸红，或是容光闪耀。而且这句很可能是一个三角恋的小故事，Alcon与Codrus都喜欢上了漂亮的Phyllis。III.76-79这一唱一和也有可能是Alcon与Codrus 的对话。

[6]Alcon与Codrus是另外两位男性的村民。

牧歌·其五

Me. 噢，Mopsus，我们好哥俩在此碰见，
为何不闲坐这榛树与榆树之间，
你，将这轻巧的芦笛吹响，
我，把那行行的诗歌轻唱。

Mo. 啊，Menalcas，你更年长，
当然就该听从你的主张。
或是在西风吹拂的摇影下乘凉，
或是我们也可以在洞穴中躲藏：
看呐，稀疏的野葡萄串，在洞口闪耀着光芒！

Me. 在我们山里这一辈，
只有那Amyntas可以跟你媲美。

Mo. 那他可是要在歌喉比赛，
胜过那Apollo的神采？

Me. 你先开始吧，Mopsus，
你可是唱过Phyllis的妖娆，
Alcon的赞美，Codrus的胡闹？
开始吧，Tityrus会帮忙照料，吃草的羊羔！

Mo. 先不唱那些——
榉树青绿色的树皮，
刻着我新作的诗意，
还有逐行标上的音调扬抑；
你得让我先把这曲子熟悉，
然后再让Amyntas来比比。

Me. lenta salix quantum pallenti cedit olivae,

puniceis humilis quantum saliunca[1] rosetis,

iudicio nostro tantum tibi cedit Amyntas.

sed tu desine plura, puer; successimus antro.

20 **Mo.** extinctum nymphae crudeli funere Daphnim

flebant; vos coryli testes et flumina nymphis;

cum complexa sui corpus miserabile nati,

atque deos atque astra vocat crudelia mater.

non ulli pastos illis egere diebus

25 frigida, Daphni, boves ad flumina; nulla neque amnem

libavit quadrupes, nec graminis attigit herbam.

Daphni, tuum Poenos[2] etiam ingemuisse leones

interitum montesque feri silvaeque loquuntur.

Daphnis et Armenias[3] curru subiungere tigres

30 instituit; Daphnis thiasos[4] inducere Bacchi[5],

et foliis lentas intexere mollibus hastas.

---

[1]saliunca是一种草本的香料植物，可能是Valeriana celtica缬草。

[2]Poeni本指罗马人的死敌迦太基人，这里可能指代非洲的狮子，也可能指狮子残忍凶暴（罗马人对迦太基人的印象）。

[3]Armenia，古国名，在罗马疆域的西北方，今Armenia，Turkey和Iran交界地。

[4]thiasus是献给酒神Bacchus的祭典舞蹈（也有其他神的thiasus记载），其间代表酒神的战车会由豹子老虎等猛兽拉动。

[5]Bacchus，酒神，即*Dionysus*。

Me. 苍青的橄榄胜过柔软的柳条，
鲜红的蔷薇远超低微的缬草，
依我看，正如你比那Amyntas高出不少。
但先打住——这洞口，我们已经来到。

Mo. nymph女神们都在痛哭不已，
是为逝去的Daphnis，他惨死的回忆，
为女神作证的，有榛丛还有山溪！
母亲抱起儿子悲凉的躯体，
哀叹着诸神与繁星的凄厉。
噢，Daphnis!
在那段日子里，
没有牧人让牛去喝冰溪；
没有四脚兽到河边嬉戏，
甚至没有去碰下那草地！
噢，Daphnis!
山野丛林把你的死讯传递，
连凶暴的非洲狮都在哀啼！
是那Daphnis，
教导我们在战车前绑上Armenia的猛虎，
是那Daphnis，
指引我们庆祝酒神Bacchus的歌舞，
给柔韧的杖，缠上软嫩的叶簇[1]。

---

[1]这个似乎说的是酒神的手杖，叫Thyrsus，杖身是Ferula communis大阿魏，一种高大的草本植物，所以说柔韧。杖上缠了常青藤叶子。这三句话三个意象其实都是说一件事情：Daphnis有可能是Bacchus的祭司。有观点认为这里Daphnis暗指被刺杀的Julius Caesar，存疑。

vitis ut arboribus decori est, ut vitibus uvae,
ut gregibus tauri, segetes ut pinguibus arvis,
tu decus omne tuis. postquam te fata tulerunt,
35　　ipsa Pales[1] agros atque ipse reliquit Apollo.
grandia saepe quibus mandavimus hordea sulcis,
infelix lolium[2] et steriles nascuntur avenae[3];
pro molli viola[4], pro purpureo narcisso,
carduus[5] et spinis surgit paliurus[6] acutis.
40　　spargite humum foliis, inducite fontibus umbras,
pastores, mandat fieri sibi talia Daphnis;
et tumulum facite, et tumulo superaddite carmen:
'Daphnis ego in siluis, hinc usque ad sidera notus,
formosi pecoris custos, formosior ipse.'

45 **Me.**　tale tuum carmen nobis, divine poeta,
quale sopor fessis in gramine, quale per aestum
dulcis aquae saliente sitim restinguere rivo.

---

[1]Pales是畜牧女神。
[2]lolium指Lolium temulentum，毒麦。
[3]avena这里指Avena fatua，野燕麦，也是杂草。
[4]参见II.47注。
[5]carduus大概是一种蓟草，叶片带尖刺。
[6]paliurus大概指Paliurus spina-christi，滨枣，一种荆棘。

正如葡萄藤为树林增光，

正如葡萄将葡萄藤点亮，

正如公牛站在兽群的中央，

正如谷子之于肥沃的土壤，

正如你是我们全部的光芒！

这命运带走了你，

连Apollo与Pales都离开了农地。

我们在田垄里播撒下饱满的大麦，

常常只有不幸的毒小麦，随地铺开，

往往还有不育的野燕麦，泛滥成灾！

没有水仙花的紫妆，没有香堇花的柔软，

带着尖刺的蓟草和荆棘却四处弥漫！

牧人[1]啊，Daphnis如此托付：

往地面撒下绿叶的青翠，

将阴影盖上清凉的泉水；

堆砌土垒，刻上墓碑：

"吾，Daphnis，

森林知晓吾名，

吾名上达群星，

群星守护水灵的羊群[2]，

羊群吾比它更加水灵。"

Me. 天启的诗人啊，

我们听到你的歌谣，

就像是劳累的牧人，在草地上的午觉，

或是甜美的泉涌，缓解了酷暑的热燥。

---

[1] 大概指Menalcas，参见IX.19-20。
[2] 原文是"我守护羊群"。

nec calamis solum aequiparas, sed voce magistrum.

fortunate puer, tu nunc eris alter ab illo.

50   nos tamen haec quocumque modo tibi nostra vicissim

dicemus, Daphnimque tuum tollemus ad astra;

Daphnin ad astra feremus: amavit nos quoque Daphnis.

Mo. an quicquam nobis tali sit munere maius?

et puer ipse fuit cantari dignus, et ista

55   iam pridem Stimichon[1] laudavit carmina nobis.

Me. candidus insuetum miratur limen Olympi[2],

sub pedibusque videt nubes et sidera Daphnis.

ergo alacris silvas et cetera rura voluptas

Panaque[3] pastoresque tenet, Dryadasque[4] puellas;

60   nec lupus insidias pecori, nec retia cervis

ulla dolum meditantur: amat bonus otia Daphnis.

ipsi laetitia voces ad sidera iactant

intonsi montes; ipsae iam carmina rupes,

ipsa sonant arbusta: 'deus, deus ille, Menalca.'

---

[1] Stimichon有可能就是上文说的那位大师。

[2] Olympus，众神的居所。

[3] *Pan*神，见II.31注。

[4] Dryadas是一种住在森林的nymph妖精，也特指橡树妖精。

你不只是笛声，
歌喉也到达了那位大师之境，
幸运的孩子啊，
你已然是第二个大师！
接下来该轮到我，尽我所能，
让Daphnis上达群星！
我们将Daphnis送上星辰，
那Daphnis也曾爱着我们！

Mo. 于我而言，又有什么比这更好的馈赠！
那男孩的确配得上诗歌传承！
很久前，连Stimichon都跟我赞美过你这歌声！

Me. 光辉的Daphnis看着脚下那群星与云层，
惊叹于这陌生的Olympus大门。
于是Pan神和牧人们都心花怒放，
还有Dryadas仙女们都欣喜若狂，
甚至连山林与田野都充满了欢畅！
恶狼不再盯着群羊，
公鹿不再惧怕猎网；
善良的Daphnis喜欢悠闲的时光！
树木繁茂的大山，
向着星空愉快地呼喊，
山岩和丛林都传递着惊叹：
"Menalcas，神，他是神啊[1]！"

---

[1]这句话没有动词，有可能指Daphnis现在是神，也有可能说他一直就是神。参见前注II.26。

65 sis bonus o felixque tuis! en quattuor aras:
ecce duas tibi, Daphni, duas altaria Phoebo[1].
pocula bina[2] novo spumantia lacte quotannis
craterasque duo statuam tibi pinguis olivi,
et multo in primis hilarans convivia Baccho[3],
70 ante focum, si frigus erit, si messis, in umbra,
vina novum fundam calathis Ariusia[4] nectar[5].
cantabunt mihi Damoetas et Lyctius[6] Aegon[7];
saltantis satyros[8] imitabitur Alphesiboeus[9].
haec tibi semper erunt, et cum solemnia vota
75 reddemus nymphis, et cum lustrabimus agros.
dum iuga montis aper, fluvios dum piscis amabit,
dumque thymo pascentur apes, dum rore cicadae,
semper honos nomenque tuum laudesque manebunt;
ut Baccho Cererique[10], tibi sic vota quotannis
80 agricolae facient: damnabis tu quoque votis.

---

[1]Phoebus，即*Apollo*。

[2]这里的两杯和下行的两碗似乎是每年祭祀两次，每次一杯奶一碗油的意思，见74-75行。

[3]Bacchus，酒神，这里指代美酒。

[4]Ariusium是希腊的Chios岛的中部山地，产葡萄和美酒。

[5]nectar是神的饮料。

[6]Lyctus是Crete岛上的一个城镇，这里指Aegon出身原是Crete岛。

[7]参见II.2，Damoeta帮Aegon看羊。

[8]satyrus即satyr，半人半羊的山神，其形象经常伴随*Pan*神与nymph仙女出现。

[9]Alphesiboeus是另外一位男性村民，在XIII中出场，与Damon斗歌。

[10]Ceres，司掌谷物的女神，即希腊神话的*Demeter*。

请你祝福你的同伴!
这里有四座祭坛,
两座是给你,Daphnis!
另外两座是给那Apollo!
我每年都要给你两次献上:
满杯泡沫的新鲜奶,
整碗清亮的橄榄油;
还要把那美酒喝够,
狂欢的饮宴,不醉不休!
天冷就在火炉前,丰收就在树荫间,
我要在酒杯中倒上,
Ariusia的美酒,新酿的琼浆!
Lyctus的Aegon和Damoetas将为我歌唱,
Alphesiboeus把satyr们的舞步模仿!
这些每年都会给你进献,
一次,当我们向nymph女神立下誓言,
一次,当我们用神圣的仪式净化农田。
鱼群喜欢那溪涧,
野猪喜欢那山巅,
蜜蜂吸食百里香,
蝉在晨露上留连——
如同这些永远都不会改变:
还有你的声名,你的荣光,对你的赞美之言!
就像对酒神Bacchus与谷神Ceres,
农夫年年向你祈祷丰收,
你也要回应他们的恳求。

Mo. quae tibi, quae tali reddam pro carmine dona?
nam neque me tantum venientis sibilus Austri[1],
nec percussa iuvant fluctu tam litora, nec quae
saxosas inter decurrunt flumina valles.

85 **Me.** hac te nos fragili donabimus ante cicuta:
haec nos, 'formosum Corydon ardebat Alexim,'
haec eadem docuit, 'cuium pecus, an Meliboei?'

Mo. at tu sume pedum[2], quod, me cum saepe rogaret,
non tulit Antigenes[3]—-et erat tum dignus amari—
90 formosum paribus nodis atque aere, Menalca.

---

[1]Auster，南风之神。

[2]pedum是牧羊人用来钩住羊的长杖，一头像一个弯钩，能钩在羊的脖子上。它是Muse之一Thalia的象征，同时也是拉丁字母"L"的原型。这里翻译为牧杖。

[3]Antigenes是另一位男性，大概也是牧人。

Mo. 听完这歌，我哪有什么可以回赠？
　　　无论是拂面而来的南风私语，
　　　或者是拍击海岸的大浪欢愉，
　　　还是乱石山谷间的溪流奏曲，
　　　都远不及你这歌那般动人心绪！

Me. 我先要赠你这柔弱的芦笛，
　　　它曾教我"牧人Corydon热恋上了美丽的Alexis[1]"，
　　　也教会我"这是谁的羊，或是Meliboeus[2]？"

Mo. Menalcas啊，请你拿着这根牧杖，
　　　Antigenes一直求我，但我一直收藏，
　　　（尽管当时他值得我爱！）
　　　你看它如此漂亮——
　　　节点均匀生长，铜饰闪闪发光！

---

[1] 见II.1。
[2] 见III.1。

ECLOGA VI

两个男孩和一位水仙子把山神捆住，让他
讲各色各样的神话故事。最后黄昏临近，二人
恋恋不舍地赶着羊群回家。

ECLOGA VI

Prima Syracosio[1] dignata est ludere versu,
nostra nec erubuit silvas habitare Thalia[2].
cum canerem reges et proelia, Cynthius[3] aurem
vellit, et admonuit: 'pastorem, Tityre, pinguis
5   pascere oportet ovis, deductum dicere carmen.'
nunc ego—namque super tibi erunt, qui dicere laudes,
Vare[4], tuas cupiant, et tristia condere bella—
agrestem tenui meditabor arundine Musam[5].
non iniussa cano. si quis tamen haec quoque, si quis
10 captus amore leget, te nostrae, Vare, myricae,
te nemus omne canet; nec Phoebo[6] gratior ulla est,
quam sibi quae Vari praescripsit pagina nomen.
pergite, Pierides[7]! Chromis et Mnasyllos in antro
Silenum[8] pueri somno videre iacentem,
15 inflatum hesterno venas, ut semper, Iaccho[9].

---

[1] Syracusae即Sicily岛上的Syracuse。Syracuse之歌指牧歌。参见IV.1。
[2] Thalia是Muse之一，司掌喜剧与牧歌。
[3] Cynthus是Delos岛上的一座山，这里指代那里出生的*Apollo*。
[4] Alfenus Varus，前39年十月之后的替补执政。似乎跟前面的Pollio一样是作者的熟人。
[5] Muse女神，这里指代诗歌。
[6] Phoebus，即*Apollo*。
[7] 指代Muse，参见III.85。
[8] Silenus是神话中酒神的导师。经常以喝醉酒的老头的形象出现。
[9] Iacchus，酒神Bacchus的别名。

牧歌·其六

最早是她，我的Thalia，
她下凡人间，把牧歌玩弄，
她屈身山林，却不会脸红。
我想歌颂君王与战火，
Apollo[1]却拽起我的耳朵，
对我训诫着说：
"Tityrus啊，作为一个牧人，
应该喂肥他的羊群，
这歌却要唱得谦逊。"
Varus啊，给你歌功颂德的人已有好多，
他们都争抢着去描绘残酷的战火；
而我，借这细长的芦管，
就把这山野的清歌把玩。
我这歌可不是随性而作：
但若有人被爱俘获；
但若有人读起这诗，
Varus，那我们的柽柳和丛林都将为你欢歌！
而你的大名若写上这书页，
没有什么比这更能让Apollo喜悦！

Muse们，开始吧！
两个男孩，Chromis和Mnasyllos，
看见山神Silenus在洞穴中睡着，
他一如既往，因为宿醉而脸色红燥。

---

[1] 所以I.6中Tityrus碰到的神可能就是*Apollo*？

serta procul tantum capiti delapsa iacebant,
et gravis attrita pendebat cantharus[1] ansa.
adgressi—nam saepe senex spe carminis ambo
luserat—iniciunt ipsis ex vincula sertis.

20 addit se sociam timidisque supervenit Aegle[2]—
Aegle, Naiadum[3] pulcherrima—iamque videnti
sanguineis frontem moris et tempora pingit.
ille dolum ridens, 'quo vincula nectitis?' inquit;
'solvite me, pueri; satis est potuisse videri:

25 carmina, quae voltis, cognoscite; carmina vobis,
huic aliud mercedis erit.' simul incipit ipse.
tum vero in numerum Faunosque[4] ferasque videres
ludere, tum rigidas motare cacumina quercus;
nec tantum Phoebo gaudet Parnasia[5] rupes,

30 nec tantum Rhodope[6] miratur et Ismarus[7] Orphea[8].
namque canebat, uti magnum per inane coacta
semina terrarumque animaeque marisque fuissent,
et liquidi simul ignis; ut his ex omnia primis,
omnia et ipse tener mundi concreverit orbis[9];

---

[1] cantharus是一种大型的酒杯，一般有两个对称的把手。
[2] Aegle是一位nymph女神，传说是*Zeus*的女儿。
[3] Nais，水之妖精，参见II.46。
[4] Faunus，牧人的保护神，被罗马人等同于*Pan*神。
[5] Parnasus是*Apollo*与Muse的圣山，Delphi与Castalia圣泉在其山脚。
[6] Rhodope是Thrace的一座高山。
[7] Ismarus山在Thrace南部海岸。
[8] 见IV.58注。
[9] orbis有很多可能的解释。按照上下文，要么是星空即天球，要么是初生的地球。

不远处是他头顶掉落的花环；

沉重的酒杯，杯柄磨得晶亮。

靠近后，他们拿花环当手铐把他捆绑——

这老头经常捉弄他们对诗歌的愿望！

看着小心翼翼的他俩，女神Aegle也过来帮忙，

Aegle！水仙女中，她有最美的模样！

她把老头的额头鬓角画上血红色的山桑，

而现在他看着恶作剧的众人，笑着问道：

"为何把我捆上？孩子们，快帮我松绑，

这已经足够证明你们很强！

来听你们想要的歌，送给你们的乐章，

而对她，则有另外的奖赏[1]。"

说完他就开始歌唱——

你看，Faunus与野兽，都依着节拍在嬉戏玩闹，

连坚实的橡树，也随着节奏摇晃着树梢！

Parnasus的重峦，

从未因Apollo而如此喜悦，

Rhodope与Ismarus山，

也从未对Orpheus如此赞叹！

他开始唱起，

在这巨大的虚空，

大地，空气，深海与纯净的火种[2]，

各种元素的种子一起汇聚其中；

这本初之物，乃万物之源头，

它们将这精细的天球，一同铸就。

---

[1]这里有很强烈的调情意味，后面作者没有再提起这事。
[2]这里就是四大元素。

35   tum durare solum et discludere Nerea[1] ponto

coeperit, et rerum paulatim sumere formas;

iamque novum terrae stupeant lucescere solem,

altius atque cadant summotis nubibus imbres;

incipiant silvae cum primum surgere cumque

40   rara per ignaros errent animalia montis.

hinc lapides Pyrrhae[2] iactos, Saturnia[3] regna,

Caucasiasque[4] refert volucres furtumque Promethei[5].

his adiungit, Hylan[6] nautae[7] quo fonte relictum

clamassent, ut litus 'Hyla, Hyla!' omne sonaret.

45   et fortunatam, si numquam armenta fuissent,

Pasiphaen[8] nivei solatur amore iuvenci.

ah, virgo infelix, quae te dementia cepit!

Proetides[9] inplerunt falsis mugitibus agros;

---

[1]Nereus是海神*Oceanus*与*Tethys*之子，众多水之妖精的父亲。这里指代海水或者水。

[2]这是神话中Deucalion与Pyrrha夫妻的故事。*Zeus*用大洪水结束了青铜时代，只剩下他们两夫妻。他们征求Delphi的神谕，结果是让他们掷出"母亲的骨头"。他们理解母亲是指大地母神*Gaia*，所以神谕是说投掷石子。然后Deucalion掷出的石子略大，变成了男人，Pyrrha掷出的稍小，变成了女人，这些就是黑铁时代的人类。原文没有"轻巧"一意。

[3]参见IV.6 注。

[4]即Caucasus山。

[5]Prometheus是Titans神族，最著名的事迹就是偷来火种给人类，自己在Caucasus山上接受惩罚，每天被老鹰啄食肝脏，后被大英雄Hercules解救。一说他是Deucalion的父亲。

[6]Hylas是神话中Hercules的同伴，著名的美少年。因其美色被水之妖精（一类nymph女神）掳走。

[7]这里的水手或者船员是指Argo船上Hylas的同伴们。

[8]Pasiphae是神话传说中Crete的王后，Minos之妻，是太阳神*Helios*与海之妖精Perse之女。她的女儿Ariadne是酒神的妻子，她因Minos触犯了海神*Poseidon*（即Neptune），被*Poseidon*诅咒，与公牛交合生下了牛头人Minotaur。

[9]Proetus是希腊古城邦Argos的国王。他的女儿们因为冒犯了酒神或者天

然后土壤开始变硬，

将水分开，聚成大海，

一点点变成这万事万物的外型；

再然后，大地惊讶于这新生的太阳，光芒万丈，

雨水从升至高空的云层中轰然而下，泽被四方；

起初，树木开始生长，

零落的动物在陌生的山间游荡。

他讲起——

Pyrrha扔出的石头轻巧，

Saturnus统治的地表，

Prometheus的偷盗，

还有Caucasus山的飞鸟。

他又说起——

走失的Hylas，是在哪处的山泉，

他的船员同伴们在向他呼喊，

"Hylas，Hylas!"的声音回荡在各处的水岸。

他还缓缓地说起——

Pasiphae爱上了雪白的公牛犊，

若从来没有过牲畜，

她本该有多么幸福!

啊，不幸的少女!

是什么让你疯狂!

Proetus的女儿们，

让田野里充满了虚假的牛吟；

后Hera而被惩罚，以为自己是牛，发疯裸奔。后被著名的医师Melampus治愈。

at non tam turpis pecudum tamen ulla secuta

50   concubitus, quamvis collo timuisset aratrum,

et saepe in levi quaesisset cornua fronte.

ah, virgo infelix, tu nunc in montibus erras;

ille, latus niveum molli fultus hyacintho[1],

ilice sub nigra pallentis ruminat herbas,

55   aut aliquam in magno sequitur grege. 'claudite, nymphae,

Dictaeae[2] nymphae, nemorum iam claudite saltus,

si qua forte ferant oculis sese obvia nostris

errabunda bovis vestigia; forsitan illum,

aut herba captum viridi, aut armenta secutum,

60   perducant aliquae stabula ad Gortynia[3] vaccae.'

tum canit Hesperidum[4] miratam mala puellam;

tum Phaethontiades[5] musco circumdat amarae[6]

corticis, atque solo proceras erigit alnos.

---

[1]参见III.63注。

[2]Dicte是Crete岛上的一座山。Zeus的父亲Cronus（即Saturnus）为了防止他的子女像他一样推翻父亲的统治，就把出生的子女一个个吞到肚子里。Zeus是最小的儿子，在他幼年时，他的母亲Rhea为了躲避Cronus将其藏在Dicte山上的一个山洞内。这里应该是指代Crete。

[3]Gortyna是Crete岛上的一个城镇，Zeus变成雪白的公牛，把美丽的Europa诱拐至此，在一棵悬铃木下交合。这里应该是反用了这个典故，说公牛被母牛拐走。

[4]首先，Hesperus即昏星，与Phosphorus晨星相对，是神话中代表金星的双子兄弟。罗马人称其为Vesper与Lucifer。后来他们被Venus代替。Hesperides指的是黄昏之妖精，是一类nymph女神。一说是夜之女神Nyx的女儿，一说是Hesperus的女儿或者孙女。她们守护着极西之处天后Hera的金苹果果园。

[5]Phaethon是太阳神Helios的儿子，驾驭太阳马车失控身死。后来他的姐妹们（Phaethontias，一说是他的女儿们）痛哭不已，伤心过度，最后变成桤树或者黑杨树，而她们的眼泪变成了琥珀。

[6]有版本作amaro，区别就是形容树皮cortex或者苔藓muscus是苦味的。

虽然她惧怕脖子会被套上犁轭，

或是常常因生怕长出牛角，

去摸索那轻盈[1]的前额，

却也从未下贱到与野兽交合！

啊，不幸的少女！

你如今在大山间放浪，

而那雪白的它却在柔软的唐菖蒲间斜躺，

在深黑的橡树下反复咀嚼[2]着泛白的草香，

或在大群的牛羊间跟着另一只母牛游荡。

"nymph女神们，Crete的nymph女神们[3]！

藏起来！把这林间的草场藏起来！

这样我或许能看见那公牛凌乱的足迹[4]，

不然它或者跟着兽群，

或者留恋于青青的草地，

或者被别的母牛带去Gortyna的牛棚里！"

然后他又唱起——

贪恋金苹果的女孩是谁[5]，

还有那Phaethon的姐妹，

她们被苦味的树皮藓包围，

拔地而起的桤树还在流泪！

---

[1] 指其实没有长出牛角，所以很轻。

[2] 牛是反刍动物。

[3] 这段话应该是Pasiphae说的。

[4] 所以要把草场藏起来，不让公牛走。

[5] 神话里关于金苹果的女孩有名的故事有两个：首先是Artemis的女猎手Atalanta，她与求婚者比赛跑步，如果胜了就可以娶她，输了就要被杀。最后Hippomenes借Aphrodite的金苹果，在赛跑中丢出，最后娶到了留恋金苹果的Atalanta；第二处是仇恨女神Eris丢出金苹果，让Hera，Athena和Aphrodite相互争夺，最后引发了Troy战争。

tum canit, errantem Permessi[1] ad flumina Gallum[2]

65 Aonas[3] in montis ut duxerit una sororum,

utque viro Phoebi[4] chorus adsurrexerit omnis;

ut Linus[5] haec illi, divino carmine pastor,

floribus atque apio crinis ornatus amaro,

dixerit: 'hos tibi dant calamos, en accipe, Musae,

70 Ascraeo[6] quos ante seni, quibus ille solebat

cantando rigidas deducere montibus ornos[7]:

his tibi Grynei[8] nemoris dicatur origo,

ne quis sit lucus quo se plus iactet Apollo.'

quid loquar aut Scyllam Nisi[9], quam fama secuta est

75 candida succinctam latrantibus inguina monstris

Dulichias[10] vexasse rates, et gurgite in alto,

ah, timidos nautas canibus lacerasse marinis.

---

[1]Permessus河是*Apollo*与Muse的圣河，在Helicon山。

[2]Gallus似乎是作者现实中的朋友，政治家Gaius Cornelius Gallus。

[3]Aonia是一个地区名，Muse的圣山Helion山就在此。

[4]Phoebus，即*Apollo*。

[5] 见IV.59注。

[6]这里指代古希腊诗人Hesiod，他出生在Helion山脚的小镇Ascra。

[7]ornus即野山杉，喜欢多岩山地；木质坚硬，可以制作武器。

[8]Grynium在今Turkey西部，有Apollo的圣林与神庙。

[9]Scylla是古希腊Megara的国王Nisus的女儿。Nisus有一束神明庇佑的紫发保护国家，但后来Scylla为情人将Nisus的紫发剪下，最后导致城破国亡。Nisus死后化为海雕，一只追逐着Scylla死后化身的水鸟。这里提到的另外一个Scylla是某种海怪，上身是人，下身是鱼尾的三头犬的形象，跟前面的Scylla应该不是同一人物。

[10]Dulichium是Ionia海上的一个海岛，在Odysseus的老家Ithaca岛附近。这里Dulichium之船应该是指代Odysseus的船。

他又唱到，
Gallus徘徊在Permessus的溪涧，
被姐妹之一[1]带到Aonia的山巅；
Apollo的乐师全体起立；
带着鲜花与苦涩欧芹的头饰，
那牧人Linus唱起神圣的歌词：
"Muse女神将这芦笛恩赐，
你来，将它收下——
这之前曾给那Ascra的老丈，
他就用这笛子歌唱，
将坚硬的野山杉带出这山岗。
你用它述说Grynium圣林的起点，
Apollo就不会在别的林子留恋。"

我为何还要提到，
他唱起Nisus的女儿Scylla，
或是那她——
白色的下身缠绕着咆哮的妖祸，
传说的海怪袭扰着Odysseus的归国，
将他的海船卷入到巨大的漩涡——
啊，那海里的凶犬，
把惊惧的水手撕成碎片！

---

[1]可能是Muse之一，或是Muse手下的nymph妖精，存疑。

aut ut mutatos Terei[1] narraverit artus;

quas illi Philomela dapes, quae dona pararit,

80   quo cursu deserta petiverit, et quibus ante

infelix sua tecta super volitaverit alis?

omnia, quae Phoebo[2] quondam meditante, beatus

audiit Eurotas[3], iussitque ediscere laurus,

ille canit: pulsae referunt ad sidera valles;

85   cogere donec ovis stabulis numerumque referre

iussit, et invito processit Vesper[4] Olympo[5].

---

[1] 希腊神话中，Tereus是Thrace的国王。他设计强奸了妻子Procne的妹妹Philomela，并割了她的舌头。后姐妹二人合谋将Tereus的儿子杀死，并做成菜肴给Tereus吃下。得知真相的Tereus追杀二人。后来三人都被变成了鸟：Procne变成了赤胸燕，Philomela变成了夜莺，而Tereus变成了戴胜鸟。

[2] Phoebus，即*Apollo*。

[3] Sparta城附近的一条大河。

[4] Vesper，即昏星，参见VI.61注。

[5] 这里指代天空。

他如何述说Tereus变幻的手臂[1]，
还有Philomela给他准备的盛宴和厚礼？
凄厉的他如何迅敏地搜寻荒地，
挥舞着翅膀，在自家屋顶上盘旋不已？

他唱过的所有诗篇[2]，
是Apollo之前将其默念，
欢乐的Eurotas河[3]也曾听遍，
这河还让月桂树[4]记在心间——
这歌声激荡在山谷，回响在星空；
他二人一直没有把羊群清点收拢，
直到昏星闪耀在恋恋不舍的天穹。

---

[1] 指变成翅膀。
[2] 一种说法是这里指前面这些诗歌都是Apollo所作。也有说，这里指另外的诗歌，Apollo所作，但是没有写出具体内容。按上下文，应该是前面的说法更符合原意。
[3] Apollo曾和Hyacinthus在Eurotas河边热恋。参见III.63。
[4] 月桂是Apollo的圣树。

ECLOGA VII

  又一场赛歌，这次是Corydon和Thyrsis。Meliboeus此时还惦记着自家的羊，但诗人们对歌的诱惑力明显更大。

ECLOGA VII

M. Forte sub arguta consederat ilice Daphnis,
compulerantque greges Corydon et Thyrsis in unum,
Thyrsis[1] ovis, Corydon distentas lacte capellas,
ambo florentes aetatibus, Arcades[2] ambo,
5 et cantare pares, et respondere parati.
huc mihi, dum teneras defendo a frigore myrtos,
vir gregis ipse caper deerraverat; atque ego Daphnim
aspicio. ille ubi me contra videt: 'ocius' inquit
'huc ades, o Meliboee, caper tibi salvus et haedi;
10 et, si quid cessare potes, requiesce sub umbra.
huc ipsi potum venient per prata iuvenci,
hic viridis tenera praetexit arundine ripas
Mincius[3], eque sacra resonant examina quercu.'
quid facerem? neque ego Alcippen[4], nec Phyllida habebam,
15 depulsos a lacte domi quae clauderet agnos,
et certamen erat, Corydon cum Thyrside, magnum.
posthabui tamen illorum mea seria ludo:
alternis igitur contendere versibus ambo
coepere; alternos Musae meminisse volebant.
20 hos Corydon, illos referebat in ordine Thyrsis.

---

[1] 这段是Meliboeus回忆两位牧人Corydon与Thyrsis的对歌。

[2] Arcadia，参见IV.41。这里很可能只是指代 "Arcadia眷恋之人"，即精通牧歌之人，参见X.31。

[3] Mincius河是Po河的支流，作者的家乡Mantua就坐落于河边。但是这个与Arcadia山对不上号，可能作者暗示这里两处山河都是虚指，指代当地的山与河，大概率还是在Sicilia。也有可能这些地名都是指有名诗人的故乡，所以是 "我们这诗词之乡" 的意思。

[4] Alcippe是一个女性的名字，大概也是村民。

牧歌·其七

M. 那日Daphnis正在碎语的橡树下闲坐，

Corydon与Thyrsis把羊群赶到一坨，

那Thyrsis带着绵羊，

Corydon则是山羊，奶水很多；

他们是风华正茂，Arcadia的小伙，

正准备开始比赛对歌。

为防冰霜，我正呵护着娇嫩的桃金娘[1]，

羊群领头，那公山羊却不知去了何方！

我见到了Daphnis，

而Daphnis也看着我说：

"快！Meliboeus，快来这树影下歇下脚，

不要担心你的公羊和羊羔！

小牛都会穿越牧场，自己来这喝个爽——

这里，Mincius河用柔嫩的芦苇盖满了绿色的河床，

这里，神圣的橡树[2]中传来蜜蜂嗡嗡的声响。"

我又能做什么？没有Alcippe或是Phyllis帮忙，

家中刚断奶的羊羔需要喂养，

但Corydon和Thyrsis的比赛可是盛事一桩！

最后我还是放下手头的正事，

去聆听两人的对诗：

于是，他们的比赛马上开始！

按照顺序，Corydon先来，Thyrsis后到：

Muse女神也喜欢回忆[3]对唱的歌谣！

---

[1] 桃金娘喜欢海岸，不太可能种植在高山Arcadia或是内陆平原Mantua。
[2] 见I.17注。
[3] Muse的母亲是记忆女神Mnemosyne。

C. nymphae, noster amor, Libethrides[1], aut mihi carmen,
quale meo Codro[2], concedite — proxima Phoebi[3]
versibus ille facit — aut, si non possumus omnes,
hic arguta sacra pendebit fistula pinu.

25 **T.** pastores, hedera crescentem ornate poetam,
Arcades — invidia rumpantur ut ilia Codro —
aut si ultra placitum laudarit, baccare[4] frontem
cingite, ne vati noceat mala lingua futuro.

C. saetosi caput hoc apri tibi, Delia[5], parvus
30 et ramosa Micon[6] vivacis cornua cervi.
si proprium hoc fuerit, levi de marmore tota
puniceo stabis suras evincta cothurno[7].

T. sinum lactis et haec te liba, Priape[8], quotannis
exspectare sat est: custos es pauperis horti.
35 nunc te marmoreum pro tempore fecimus; at tu,
si fetura gregem suppleverit, aureus esto.

---

[1]Libethra是在Macedonia的一处泉水，是Muse女神的圣泉。传说中也是Orpheus的出生地。这里Libethrides是Muse的别名。

[2]Codrus，另一位男性村民，V.10-11与Alcon和Phyllis有段小故事。

[3]Pheobus，即*Apollo*。

[4]参见IV.22注。

[5]指*Artemis*，即Diana，参见III.67。

[6]见III.10，Micon的果树被Damoetas砍伤。

[7]这是希腊式的高脚靴，悲剧演员一般会穿着它。脚背和小腿前方裸露，用鞋带交叉捆绑扎紧，所以这里用了evincio这个动词。

[8]Priapus是园艺之神，也是生殖与养蜂之神。最普遍的说法认为他是酒神Bacchus之子。

C.　Libethra的女神，我爱的Muse啊！
　　要么，请赐我如Codrus一般的歌咏，
　　（他能唱最接近Apollo的诗句！）
　　要么，若是我们都不中用，
　　就把我这清亮的芦笛挂上神圣的青松！

T.　Arcadia的牧羊人啊，
　　要么，给冉冉升起的诗人装饰上常青藤，
　　（让Codrus的嫉妒涨破肚皮！）
　　要么，若是他夸奖过盛，
　　请用仙客来环绕前庭[1]，
　　这样恶意的中伤就不会损害未来的诗圣。

C.　Diana！卑微的Micon给你献祭，
　　这野猪头，绒毛整齐，
　　这老鹿角，分叉细密；
　　若是你对这特殊的礼物十分满意，
　　那么你大理石的神像将光滑无比，
　　绑着鲜红长靴的双足将亭亭玉立。

T.　Priapus！你是贫乏花园的守护，
　　那每年收到些蛋糕和一碗奶也该满足！
　　现在我们暂时给你造大理石像，
　　若是兽群繁衍，可以换上金装。

---

[1]指额头。

C. Nerine[1] Galatea[2], thymo mihi dulcior Hyblae[3],

candidior cycnis, hedera formosior alba[4],

cum primum pasti repetent praesepia tauri,

40 si qua tui Corydonis habet te cura, venito.

T. immo ego Sardoniis[5] videar tibi amarior herbis[6],

horridior rusco[7], proiecta vilior alga,

si mihi non haec lux toto iam longior anno est.

ite domum pasti, si quis pudor, ite iuvenci[8].

45 **C.** muscosi fontes et somno mollior herba,

et quae vos rara viridis tegit arbutus umbra,

solstitium pecori defendite; iam venit aestas

torrida, iam lento turgent in palmite gemmae.

T. hic focus et taedae[9] pingues, hic plurimus ignis

50 semper, et adsidua postes fuligine nigri;

hic tantum Boreae[10] curamus frigora, quantum

aut numerum lupus, aut torrentia flumina ripas.

---

[1]指Nereus，参见VI.35。

[2]Galatea本是海神Nereus之女，水之妖精，与凡人Acis相恋。她经常在Sicily出现，导致这里的Cyplops独眼巨人Polyphemus因嫉妒而杀死了Acis，最后Galatea将Acis变成了Sicily的一条河流。这里可能是村里那个Galatea，诗人将其比作海神之女。

[3]Hybla山，参见I.55注。

[4]某些品种的常青藤叶子边缘会发白。

[5]即Sardinia岛。

[6]这里也提示Galatea应该是村民，而这段也就是Galatea对Corydon示爱的回应。

[7]ruscum指Ruscus aculeatus，假叶树，也叫百劳金雀花。是传统的一味草药，而屠夫也用来清理案板。

[8]iuvencus也可以指年轻人，可能Galatea只是嫌弃Corydon太年轻。

[9]taeda是一种松树，富含松脂，易燃，常作为火把或者燃料。

[10]Boreas，北风之神。

C. Galatea，宛若海神之女！于我而言，
   你比Hybla的百里香更甜蜜，
   你比天鹅更白皙，
   你比白边的常青藤更美丽！
   当吃饱的公牛回到牛棚休息，
   过来吧，若你的Corydon[1] 还在你的心里！

T. 噢，不，我看你，
   比Sardinia的草药还要苦，
   比屠夫的假叶树还要粗，
   比散落的海草还要俗！
   看着你，这白天过得跟一整年一般漫长！
   回家去吧，若是还知羞耻，回家吧，牛羊！

C. 满布青苔的泉眼，
   柔软如梦的草间；
   绿色的野莓树，阴影稀疏，
   请保护兽群度过夏至酷暑；
   炙热的盛夏天，在此驻足，
   欢乐的葡萄枝，嫩芽冒出。

T. 我这有炉子和富油的松枝，
   这里有不灭的火焰，门柱满是黑渍。
   寒冷的北风之神之于我，
   就如同羊群的数量之于狼，
   或是河岸之于汹涌的大江。

---

[1]所以Corydon喜欢Galatea，那之前Galatea可能就是Amaryllis的姐姐，最后Corydon娶了妹妹，忍受着她的傲气与娇气（II.14）；而Damon娶了Galatea。

C. stant et iuniperi, et castaneae hirsutae;
   strata iacent passim sua quaque sub arbore poma;
55   omnia nunc rident: at si formosus Alexis[1]
   montibus his abeat, videas et flumina sicca.

T. aret ager; vitio moriens sitit aeris herba;
   Liber[2] pampineas invidit collibus umbras;
   Phyllidis adventu nostrae nemus omne virebit,
60   Iuppiter et laeto descendet plurimus imbri.

C. populus Alcidae[3] gratissima, vitis Iaccho[4],
   formosae myrtus Veneri[5], sua laurea Phoebo[6];
   Phyllis amat corylos: illas dum Phyllis amabit,
   nec myrtus vincet corylos, nec laurea Phoebi.

65 **T.** fraxinus in silvis pulcherrima, pinus in hortis,
   populus in fluviis, abies in montibus altis:
   saepius at si me, Lycida[7] formose, revisas,
   fraxinus in silvis cedat tibi, pinus in hortis.

---

[1] 参见II。
[2] Liber是酒神的别名。
[3] Alceus的后代，这里特指其孙Hercules。
[4] Iachuus即Bacchus。
[5] Venus，爱神。
[6] Phoebus，即*Apollo*。
[7] Lycidas应该是一位男性的村民。

C. 刺柏和毛绒绒的栗子树林立，
　　树下到处是各自的果实遍地；
　　如今万物都在欢腾不已，
　　但若Alexis从这大山远离，
　　那你就能看到干涸的小溪。

T. 因这恶毒的空气，
　　田野干旱至极，
　　草地奄奄一息，
　　连Bacchus他自己，
　　都不给丘陵带去葡萄的荫蔽[1]；
　　但若Phyllis在此留步，
　　所有的林间都将变成绿谷——
　　最伟大的Juppiter，
　　即将降下欢畅的雨露。

C. 酒神Bacchus最爱葡萄，Hercules最喜欢白杨，
　　Apollo爱月桂，美艳的Venus喜欢桃金娘；
　　Phyllis爱着榛树——
　　啊，只要Phyllis爱着榛树，
　　那跟榛树一比，
　　桃金娘和Apollo的月桂就不值一提。

T. 灰木在林间最美，庭园中则是青松，
　　河岸边那是白杨，高山要看银冷杉。
　　美丽的Lycidas啊，若是你多来见我，
　　那林间灰木和园中青松都比你不过。

---

[1]指树叶枯死。

M. haec memini, et victum frustra contendere Thyrsim.

70 ex illo Corydon Corydon est tempore nobis.

M. 这些就是我的记忆，

　　　Thyrsis已经败了，再争也没有用。

　　　从那之后，就只有Corydon，

　　　我们的Corydon[1]！

---

[1]Thyrsis在其他章节没有被提及，也许是邻村的歌手。所以这里特别指是
"我们的" Corydon，而这比赛也是本村和邻村之间的较量。

ECLOGA VIII

  Damon和Alphesiboeus分别讲了关于爱情的故事。前者是Mopsus因为妻子背叛而跳海自尽；后者是一位少女因为热恋Daphnis而迷上了神秘术；二者有异曲同工之妙。

ECLOGA VIII

Pastorum Musam[1] Damonis et Alphesiboei[2]—
immemor herbarum quos est mirata iuvenca
certantis, quorum stupefactae carmine lynces,
et mutata suos requierunt flumina cursus—
5 Damonis Musam dicemus et Alphesiboei.
tu mihi, seu magni superas iam saxa Timavi[3],
sive oram Illyrici[4] legis aequoris, en erit umquam
ille dies, mihi cum liceat tua dicere facta?
en erit ut liceat totum mihi ferre per orbem
10 sola Sophocleo[5] tua carmina digna cothurno?
a te principium, tibi desinam: accipe iussis
carmina coepta tuis, atque hanc sine tempora circum
inter victrices hederam tibi serpere lauros[6].
frigida vix caelo noctis decesserat umbra,
15 cum ros in tenera pecori gratissimus herba;
incumbens tereti Damon sic coepit olivae.

---

[1]这里指代诗歌。

[2]这篇记录的是Damon与Alphesiboeus的赛歌，但不是相互的对歌形式，而是Damon先全部唱完，然后Alphesiboeus接下来唱。

[3]Timavus河，今名Timavo河，在今Italy与Slovenia交界的Trieste西北。

[4]Illyrii指居住在古希腊的西北方，Adriatic海北岸的部落民族。这里指代Adriatic海。

[5]Sophocles是古希腊著名的三大悲剧诗人之一，所以穿着cothurnus。参见VII.32注。

[6]6-13行是给某人的献辞。可能是Augustus，也有说指Pollio，存疑。

牧歌·其八

牧人Damon与Alphesiboeus的歌谣——
小母牛听得入迷，忘了吃草，
猞猁们也被这歌声倾倒，
小溪也居然停了下来，改变了河道——
让我们唱响Damon与Alphesiboeus的歌谣！

你现在无论是要穿越Timavus河的乱石滩，
还是航行在Adriatic海的海岸——
啊，何日我才能述说你的丰碑，
啊，何时这赞歌才能响彻宇内，
唯有这赞歌可以跟Sophocles的悲剧媲美！
我以你为起始，也以你为终结[1]：
请收下这遵命而著的诗页，
允许你那满是胜利的月桂冠，
再加缠上这常青藤的绿叶！

那夜晚的寒影，刚从清朗的天空悄然退场，
这幼嫩的草地，牲畜最喜的朝露闪着微光；
Damon就倚靠在光滑的橄榄树边[2]，开始歌唱。

---

[1] "以你为始终"和"遵命而著"两件事似乎都是指向《农事诗》，不知
为何这段文字到了这里。

[2] 一说Damon支着橄榄树枝做的牧杖。

D. nascere, praeque diem veniens age, Lucifer[1], almum,
coniugis indigno Nisae[2] deceptus amore
dum queror, et divos, quamquam nil testibus illis
20 profeci, extrema moriens tamen adloquor hora.
incipe Maenalios[3] mecum, mea tibia, versus.

D. Maenalus argutumque nemus pinosque loquentis
semper habet; semper pastorum ille audit amores,
Panaque, qui primus calamos non passus inertis.
25 incipe Maenalios mecum, mea tibia, versus.

D. Mopso Nisa datur! quid non speremus amantes?
iungentur iam grypes[4] equis, aevoque sequenti
28 cum canibus timidi venient ad pocula dammae.
28a incipe Maenalios mecum, mea tibia, versus.[5]

29 **D.** Mopse, novas incide faces[6]: tibi ducitur uxor;
30 sparge, marite, nuces: tibi deserit Hesperus Oetam[7].
incipe Maenalios mecum, mea tibia, versus.

---

[1]Lucifer，指晨星，参见IV.61注。小雅《大东》：东有启明，西有长庚。
[2]Nisa是一个女子的名字。
[3]Maenalus是*Pan*神的故乡Arcadia的一座山，也有同名的小城，后毁于战火，这里指Arcadia的牧歌。
[4]gryps，即狮鹫，有狮子的身体和老鹰的头和翅膀，会飞。
[5]有些版本缺此行。
[6]这里fax指的是婚礼上在新娘前面引路的火炬。
[7]Oeta是希腊中部的一座山，Hercules在这里自焚升天。

D. 启明星啊，请显现！

在前方引导这收获幸福的一天！

但这爱却被吾妻[1]Nisa的不贞所欺骗！

我在此哀哭，尽管神明见证并没有给我带来幸福，

我在此倾诉，向着神明说出我这将死之人的痛苦！

——我的骨笛，随我一起，开启Arcadia的音符[2]！

D. Arcadia总有那细语的丛林与松树，

Arcadia总是倾听牧人爱意的吐露，

它还有那Pan神，是他最早让芦笛不再孤独。

——我的骨笛，随我一起，开启Arcadia的乐谱！

D. Nisa嫁给了Mopsus！

世间之爱，又为什么要蹈矩循规？

胆怯的母鹿也会来跟狗一道喝水，

时代在变，狮鹫也能和骏马配对！

——我的骨笛，随我一起，开启Arcadia的光辉！

D. Mopsus啊，去砍点木头当火炬：

是那火炬为你引领新娘的步履！

新郎啊，请撒下坚果干：

昏星为你移出了Oeta山[3]！

——我的骨笛，随我一起，开启Arcadia的浪漫！

---

[1]按照前面的对歌体例，这里不是唱本人的事情。按照后文，可能是Mopsus的故事。也可能说的是Mopsus情敌的故事，那"吾妻"应作"情人"。

[2]除了最后一节，每节的末句都是一样的，但是Damon这里按照韵脚翻译成不同的词。

[3]这似乎是句谚语，类似于"日落西山"，大概意思是说夜晚已降临，新郎的愿望已经达成。

D. o digno coniuncta viro, dum despicis omnes,
　　dumque tibi est odio mea fistula, dumque capellae,
　　hirsutumque supercilium promissaque barba,
35　　nec curare deum credis mortalia quemquam!
　　incipe Maenalios mecum, mea tibia, versus.

D. saepibus in nostris parvam te roscida mala—
　　dux ego vester eram—vidi cum matre legentem.
　　alter ab undecimo tum me iam acceperat annus;
40　　iam fragilis poteram a terra contingere ramos.
　　ut vidi, ut perii! ut me malus abstulit error!
　　incipe Maenalios mecum, mea tibia, versus.

D. nunc scio, quid sit Amor[1]: duris in cotibus illum
　　aut Tmaros[2], aut Rhodope[3], aut extremi Garamantes[4],
45　　nec generis nostri puerum nec sanguinis edunt.
　　incipe Maenalios mecum, mea tibia, versus.

D. saevus Amor docuit natorum sanguine matrem[5]
　　commaculare manus; crudelis tu quoque, mater:

---

[1]这里是拟人化的概念爱神，或是特指Venus之子，小爱神Cupido，其形象经常是一个小男孩。

[2]Tmaros山在希腊Eprius。

[3]Rhodope山在Thrace。

[4]Garamantes远在非洲内陆，今Libya。

[5]这里应该说的是神话中Medea的故事。她是太阳神*Helios*的孙女，有强大的魔力。被丈夫Jason背叛，由爱生恨，将两个亲生儿子杀死。

D. 噢，爱妻，你有如此相配的夫婿！
你却看不起所有人，看不起我的笛曲，
看不起我的山羊，
看不起我密密的眉毛和长长的胡须，
你也不相信天神会关心凡间的男女！
——我的骨笛，随我一起，开启Arcadia的音律！

D. 那个紧跟着母亲的小姑娘，
我带着你们到我家篱笆墙，
采摘布满露珠的野果芳香——
这便是我们的初次相见，
我那时还是刚过十一的懵懂少年，
站在地上，刚能够到那柔枝之间；
我如何看着你！如何心荡神移！
如何这厄运的爱意，深深地植入我的心里！
——我的骨笛，随我一起，开启Arcadia的诗意！

D. 我现在知道了爱神是谁：
Tmaros山，Rhodope山，或是遥远的Garamantes，
将它生于坚硬的山石磊磊！
这个孩子[1]既非我们的族类，
也没有流淌着我们的血水！
——我的骨笛，随我一起，开启Arcadia的诗会！

D. 残忍的爱神，还让母亲，
用儿子的鲜血将双手沾染；
母亲啊，你也是一样凶残！

---

[1]指小爱神Cupido。

　　　　crudelis mater magis, an puer improbus ille?
50　　　improbus ille puer; crudelis tu quoque, mater.
　　　　incipe Maenalios mecum, mea tibia, versus.

D.　　nunc et ovis ultro fugiat lupus; aurea durae
　　　　mala ferant quercus; narcisso floreat alnus;
　　　　pinguia corticibus sudent electra myricae;
55　　　certent et cycnis ululae; sit Tityrus Orpheus[1],
　　　　Orpheus in silvis, inter delphinas Arion[2].
　　　　incipe Maenalios mecum, mea tibia, versus.

D.　　omnia vel medium fiat mare: vivite, silvae!
　　　　praeceps aerii specula de montis in undas
60　　　deferar; extremum hoc munus morientis habeto.
　　　　desine Maenalios, iam desine, tibia, versus.

　　　　haec Damon: vos, quae responderit Alphesiboeus,
　　　　dicite, Pierides[3]; non omnia possumus omnes.

A.　　effer aquam, et molli cinge haec altaria vitta[4],
65　　　verbenasque[5] adole pinguis et mascula tura[6],

---

[1] 参见III.46。
[2] Arion是传说中的人物，著名的诗人和歌手，曾被一只海豚所救。
[3] 指代Muse，参见III.85。
[4] vitta是一种窄条头巾，后演变成头环。这里用类似的布料环绕祭坛。
[5] verbena可以是各种树木的树枝树叶，在祭典时焚烧用，这里似乎是某种魔法仪式。
[6] tura即乳香，一种香料。

是这母亲更凶残，还是这孩子[1]更加不善！
这孩子是不善，但你这母亲也是凶残！
——我的骨笛，随我一起，开启Arcadia的感叹！

D. 如今，让凶狼见了羊还会逃跑，
让坚硬的橡树结出金色的蜜桃，
让柽柳的树皮分泌晶莹的琥珀，
让轻盈的桤木开满水仙的花苞！
让猫头鹰与天鹅比赛歌喉与音调，
让那Tityrus也与Orpheus试比高——
让他像Orpheus，在林间奔跑，
让他像Arion，在海豚间闪耀！
——我的骨笛，随我一起，开启Arcadia的辞藻！

D. 让万物都感受大海的咆哮！
山林，你要过得好好！
让我，从这高山之巅一头跃入波涛，
让她收下我这将死之人最后的回报——
——我的骨笛，停下来吧，停下Arcadia的歌谣！

这些就是Damon的歌集，
而Alphesiboeus的回礼——
Muse啊，这活要交给你；
每个人都会有力所不及[2]！

A. 拿出清水，用羊毛巾将祭坛环绕，
点燃多油的香枝条和雄浑的乳香料；

---

[1] 指小爱神Cupido。
[2] 原文是"不是所有人都会所有的事情。"

coniugis ut magicis sanos avertere sacris
experiar sensus nihil hic nisi carmina desunt.
ducite ab urbe domum, mea carmina, ducite Daphnim.

A. carmina vel caelo possunt deducere Lunam[1];
70　　carminibus Circe[2] socios mutavit Ulixi[3];
frigidus in pratia cantando rumpitur anguis.
ducite ab urbe domum, mea carmina, ducite Daphnim.

A. terna tibi haec primum triplici diversa colore
licia circumdo, terque haec altaria circum
75　　effigiem duco: numero deus impare gaudet.
ducite ab urbe domum, mea carmina, ducite Daphnim.

A. necte tribus nodis ternos, Amarylli, colores,
necte, Amarylli, modo, et 'Veneris[4]' dic 'vincula necto.'
ducite ab urbe domum, mea carmina, ducite Daphnim.

80　**A.** limus ut hic durescit et haec ut cera liquescit
uno eodemque igni, sic nostro Daphnis amore.
sparge molam[5], et fragilis incende bitumine laurus.
Daphnis me malus urit, ego hanc in Daphnide laurum.
ducite ab urbe domum, mea carmina, ducite Daphnim.

---

[1]Luna，即月神Selene。*Pan*神有勾引Selene的记录，而女巫Medea也会使用咒语，导致月食。

[2]Circe是神话中的精通草药与魔法的女神，会用魔药将人变成动物。在*Odyssey*中，她用歌声迷惑勾引了船员，并把他们变成了猪。

[3]Ulixes，即Odysseus。

[4]Venus，爱神。

[5]mola原意是磨石，这里指粗磨的谷物与盐的混合物（一说是制成的类似蛋糕的食物），祭祀的时候撒在祭品动物的身上。

我要用这魔法献祭找回爱人的怀抱，

除了歌声[1]，其他什么都不需要！

——我的歌声，接Daphnis从城里回家，接他回家。

A. 用这歌声，甚至能让月神下凡，

用这歌声，Circe迷惑了Odysseus的同伴，

用这歌声，能将草地上冰冷的蛇震成几段[2]！

——我的歌声，接Daphnis从城里回家，接他回家。

A. 首先，我用三色的三条线加缠，

拿起你的偶像，在祭坛环绕三圈：

是奇数[3]，天神就喜欢！

——我的歌声，接Daphnis从城里回家，接他回家。

A. Amaryllis，把这三色的线打成结，

Amaryllis，要同时说：

"我要绑上爱神的枷锁。"

——我的歌声，接Daphnis从城里回家，接他回家。

A. 在同一炉火，黏土变硬，蜡融土锅，

在同一炉火，Daphnis也被我的爱所包裹。

双手铺撒，神圣的粗面灰，

沥青焚烧，脆响的干月桂。

那坏透的家伙，Daphnis燃烧着我，

我也要用这月桂，把Daphnis烧灼！

——我的歌声，接Daphnis从城里回家，接他回家。

---

[1]这里以及下文的carmen也有咒语的意思。

[2]有可能指女巫Angitia，会用魔法迷惑蛇。

[3]Pythagoras学派似乎认为3很完美很重要；希腊神话里也经常有各种的三女神，Muse则是九姐妹。

85 **A.** talis amor Daphnim, qualis cum fessa iuvencum
        per nemora atque altos quaerendo bucula lucos
        propter aquae rivum viridi procumbit in ulva,
        perdita, nec serae meminit decedere nocti,
        talis amor teneat, nec sit mihi cura mederi.
90   ducite ab urbe domum, mea carmina, ducite Daphnim.

    A. has olim exuvias mihi perfidus ille reliquit,
        pignora cara sui, quae nunc ego limine in ipso,
        Terra, tibi mando; debent haec pignora Daphnim.
        ducite ab urbe domum, mea carmina, ducite Daphnim.

95 **A.** has herbas atque haec Ponto[1] mihi lecta venena
        ipse dedit Moeris[2]; nascuntur plurima Ponto.
        his ego saepe lupum fieri et se condere silvis
        Moerim, saepe animas imis excire sepulcris,
        atque satas alio vidi traducere messis.
100   ducite ab urbe domum, mea carmina, ducite Daphnim.

    A. fer cineres, Amarylli, foras, rivoque fluenti
        transque caput iace, nec respexeris. his ego Daphnim
        adgrediar, nihil ille deos, nil carmina curat.
        ducite ab urbe domum, mea carmina, ducite Daphnim.

---

[1]Pontus原是海神名，如果指海那是黑海，如果是陆地，那是黑海南岸的一块区域。

[2]Moeris大概也是村民，精通巫术。

A. 让Daphnis被这爱意侵蚀：
如同那小母牛在丛林间寻找相思，
筋疲力尽，倾倒在溪水边的绿植，
为爱绝望，深夜都忘了回家觅食——
让如此的爱意将Daphnis吞噬，
让我不要关心他的生死！
——我的歌声，接Daphnis从城里回家，接他回家。

A. 背信之人曾给我留下诸多幸福，
这些曾经是他爱情誓言的信物，
现在我要通通丢出，
丢出门外，丢给大地之母！
欠我一个Daphnis，这些信物！
——我的歌声，接Daphnis从城里回家，接他回家。

A. 这些野草，还有在Pontus遍地生长的毒药材，
都是Moeris亲自从Pontus给我采摘；
我常见Moeris他用这药变成狼豺，
还能遁身藏入密林之海，
从最深的墓地召唤鬼怪，
让田间的丰收变成他人之财！
——我的歌声，接Daphnis从城里回家，接他回家。

A. Amaryllis，把这些灰带出门庭，
朝着流动的小溪，把它扔过你的头顶，
千万不要回头！这样我就能把Daphnis触碰！
即使他不信神，也不关心我的歌声！
——我的歌声，接Daphnis从城里回家，接他回家。

105   **A.** aspice, corripuit tremulis altaria flammis
        sponte sua, dum ferre moror, cinis ipse: bonum sit!
        nescio quid certe est, et Hylas[1] in limine latrat.
        credimus, an, qui amant, ipsi sibi somnia fingunt?
        parcite, ab urbe venit, iam carmina, parcite, Daphnis.

---

[1]这是一只狗的名字，有现代的版本修订为Hylax。

A. 看！祭坛上的灰烬自行复燃起耀眼的火光[1]，
看来我稍等片刻，等来了上天的恩赏！
虽不能完全确定，但Hylas在门口叫得汪汪！
我们是该相信这卦象？
还是陷入爱恋之人会把自己送入梦乡？
——我的歌声，停下吧，停下，Daphnis刚从城里回家。

---

[1]死灰复燃可能是提示这里Daphnis已经去世。

ECLOGA IX

　　Menalcas的歌声似乎留住了部分的土地。两位牧人Moeris和Lycidas回忆起一些旧时的歌词，但是时间又似乎消磨了一切的情思。

ECLOGA IX

L. uo te, Moeri[1], pedes? an, quo via ducit, in urbem?

M. o Lycida, vivi pervenimus, advena nostri,
     —quod numquam veriti sumus—ut possessor agelli
     diceret: 'haec mea sunt; veteres migrate coloni!'
5   nunc victi, tristes, quoniam Fors[2] omnia versat,
     hos illi—quod nec vertat bene—mittimus haedos.

L. certe equidem audieram, qua se subducere colles
     incipiunt, mollique iugum demittere clivo,
     usque ad aquam et veteres—iam fracta cacumina—fagos
10   omnia carminibus vestrum servasse Menalcan[3].

M. audieras, et fama fuit; sed carmina tantum
     nostra valent, Lycida, tela inter Martia[4], quantum
     Chaonias[5] dicunt aquila veniente columbas.
     quod nisi me quacumque novas incidere lites
15   ante sinistra cava monuisset ab ilice cornix[6],
     nec tuus hic Moeris, nec viveret ipse Menalcas.

---

[1]这首是两个牧人Moeris和Lycidas的对话。Lycidas是VII里Thyrsis暗恋的对象；Moeris则在VIII中提到，精通巫术。

[2]Fors是命运的概念神化。

[3]Menalcas是II中Corydon备选的恋人之一，皮肤黝黑，在III与V中跟别人对歌。

[4]Mars，战神。

[5]Chaonia，古希腊的一个地区，Dodona橡树圣林和神王Zeus的神谕在此。男女祭司的名称似乎跟鸽子有关，可能来源于古代当地鸽子的神话。

[6]参见I.18。

牧歌·其九

L. Moeris，你这是去哪？
或是沿着大路进城？

M. 噢，Lycidas，
我们居然能活着见到这古怪，
以前从未担心过这一载：
异乡人占据了我们小小的田块！
他还说："这都是我的，原先的农户搬开！"
失败，悲哀，命运将一切毁坏！
我正送这些羊羔给他——愿他气数已衰！

L. 但是我可听说，
从那开始慢慢变成缓坡的高丘，
一直到水边老榉林残破的枯朽，
这些都靠你们的Menalcas用歌声得以保留？

M. Lycidas啊，是的，的确有这流言虚影；
但我们的歌声要去对抗战神Mars的刀兵，
就像是Chaonia的鸽子面对来袭的雄鹰！
要不是厄运的乌鸦在橡树洞中给我提醒，
让我不要参和最近那些争鸣，
你的Menalcas和Moeris估计早就没了性命！

L.   heu, cadit in quemquam tantum scelus? heu, tua nobis
paene simul tecum solatia rapta, Menalca?
quis caneret nymphas; quis humum florentibus herbis
20   spargeret, aut viridi fontes induceret umbra?
vel quae sublegi tacitus tibi carmina nuper,
cum te ad delicias ferres, Amaryllida, nostras?
'Tityre, dum redeo—brevis est via—pasce capellas,
et potum pastas age, Tityre, et inter agendum
25   occursare capro, cornu ferit ille, caveto.'

M.   immo haec, quae Varo[1] necdum perfecta canebat:
'Vare, tuum nomen, superet modo Mantua[2] nobis—
Mantua, vae miserae nimium vicina Cremonae[3]—
cantantes sublime ferent ad sidera cycni.'

30   **L.**   sic tua Cyrneas fugiant examina taxos[4];
sic cytiso pastae distendant ubera vaccae!
incipe, si quid habes: et me fecere poetam
Pierides[5]; sunt et mihi carmina; me quoque dicunt
vatem pastores, sed non ego credulus illis.
35   nam neque adhuc Vario[6] videor, nec dicere Cinna[7]
digna, sed argutos inter strepere anser olores.

---

[1]Varus，参见VI.7注。

[2]Mantua是作者的故乡，在安置老兵的征地运动里可能受到波及。

[3]Cremona是Po河流域的大城市，作者曾在此学习。这里是征地运动里波及严重的地区。

[4]taxus即Taxus baccata，红豆杉，有毒。参见《农事诗》IV.47。

[5]指代Muse，参见III.85。

[6]指Lucius Varius，作者同时代的诗人。

[7]也是作者同时代的诗人Gaius Helvius Cinna，可能在Julius Caesar的葬礼上被认为是Cornelius Cinna而被误杀，存疑。

L. 呜呼！谁遭过如此的恶报？

呜呼！Menalcas！

你给我们的抚慰差点被掠夺，同你一道！

谁又能歌唱nymph女神的容貌？

谁又能向大地撒下花香的野草[1]？

谁又能给泉水铺上绿影的树梢？

或是我最近偷偷听到你的歌谣，

正当你把我的甜心Amaryllis寻找！

　"Tityrus，帮我喂下羊，我去去就回，

喂饱之后，要赶它们去喝水，

赶的时候，小心别跟公羊怼，

Tityrus，它的犄角很尖锐！"

M. 比不上他为Varus作的这首，不过还没写完：

　"Varus，高歌的天鹅将把你的名字带上星辰，

但只要你把Mantua留给我们！

啊，Mantua！你太靠近Cremona的厄运！"

L. 让你的蜂群远离Cyrnos[2]的红豆杉，

让你的母牛吃上苜蓿，乳房胀大！

你先开始吧，无论你有什么想唱：

Muse女神让我做诗人，我也写过几行，

牧民们也称我为诗人，但我总怕他们瞎讲——

去跟Varius或是Cinna比歌，我真不敢当，

我就像一只灰雁[3]，在天鹅的妙曲间嘎嘎乱响。

---

[1] 参见V.40。

[2] Cyrnos，即Corsica岛。

[3] anser，即goose，在中文语境里的鹅是驯化后的大雁，而在欧洲则是驯化的灰雁。

M. id quidem ago et tacitus, Lycida, mecum ipse voluto,
si valeam meminisse; neque est ignobile carmen:
'huc ades, o Galatea; quis est nam ludus in undis?
40 hic ver purpureum; varios hic flumina circum
fundit humus flores; hic candida populus antro
imminet, et lentae texunt umbracula vites.
huc ades: insani feriant sine litora fluctus.'

L. quid, quae te pura solum sub nocte canentem
45 audieram? numeros memini, si verba tenerem.
'Daphni, quid antiquos signorum suspicis ortus?
ecce Dionaei[1] processit Caesaris astrum[2],
astrum, quo segetes gauderent frugibus, et quo
duceret apricis in collibus uva colorem.
50 insere, Daphni, piros: carpent tua poma nepotes.'

M. omnia fert aetas, animum[3] quoque: saepe ego longos
cantando puerum memini me condere soles:
nunc oblita mihi tot carmina; vox quoque Moerim
iam fugit ipsa; lupi[4] Moerim videre priores.
55 sed tamen ista satis referet tibi saepe Menalcas.

---

[1]Dione，可能是*Oceanus*和*Tethys*之女，也有可能是*Gaia*和*Uranus*之女，第十三位*Titans*神。有一种传言她是爱神Venus（*Aphrodite*）的母亲，但根据更普遍的意见，*Aphrodite*是由*Uranus*被割下的生殖器所化生。这里指Julius Caesar是Venus之子Aeneas的后裔。

[2]Caesar之星，是一颗非周期彗星。在前44年春夏出现，为Augustus神化Caesar提供了非常强力的支持，让世人认为Caesar是一位神祇。据《汉书》："元帝初元……五年四月，彗星出西北"。

[3]这里animus应该指记忆。

[4]被狼先看见了，可能是牧民间某种谚语，表示倒了霉运。

M.　我确有此意，却之不恭——
　　　而且，Lycidas啊，我刚自己还在默默背诵，
　　　若我记得不差，这歌也不算平庸：
　　　"噢，Galatea[1]，来这里吧！
　　　那浪花有什么好玩？
　　　这里有闪亮的春色流转，
　　　这里有河边的野花纷繁，
　　　这里有白杨在洞外伸展，
　　　这里有纤柔的藤蔓影斑；
　　　来这里吧，这里没有巨浪拍打着海岸！"

L.　我曾听你在清朗的深夜吟唱，
　　　我记得节奏，但拿不准歌词：
　　　"噢，Daphnis！你为何将古老的星辰仰望！
　　　看那爱神的后裔，Caesar之星在书写华章！
　　　这星让谷子在麦田里欢畅，
　　　这星让葡萄闪耀着山间落日的光芒！
　　　噢，Daphnis！去嫁接梨子，
　　　这样你的后代能收获果实！"

M.　时间消磨了一切的肉身，
　　　岁月侵蚀了有趣的灵魂。
　　　我记得小时候那终日歌唱的男孩，
　　　而如今他已忘却许许多多的挚爱；
　　　现在连Moeris的嗓音也要飞走！
　　　是不是Moeris先被那狼群回眸？
　　　但那Menalcas会为你唱个够。

---

　　　[1]这个Galatea大概是海神Nereus之女，水之妖精。参见VII.37。

L. causando nostros in longum ducis amores:
et nunc omne tibi stratum silet aequor, et omnes,
aspice, ventosi ceciderunt murmuris aurae.
hinc adeo media est nobis via; namque sepulcrum
60   incipit adparere Bianoris[1]: hic ubi densas
agricolae stringunt frondes, hic, Moeri, canamus;
hic haedos depone: tamen veniemus in urbem.
aut si, nox pluviam ne colligat ante, veremur,
cantantes licet usque—minus via laedit—eamus;
65   cantantes ut eamus, ego hoc te fasce levabo.

M. desine plura, puer, et quod nunc instat agamus:
carmina tum melius, cum venerit ipse, canemus.

---

[1]Bianor是传说中Mantua城的建立者。

L. 你的托词更引起了我爱慕的感情，
你看这所有的水面为你影湛波平，
你看这所有的天空为你风止云清。
我们刚走了一半的路程，
前面就看见Bianor之陵；
Moeris啊，
在这里，农夫们在修剪浓密的树叶，
在这里，让我们停下小羊，
在这里，让我们放声歌唱，
我们之后再进城也不忙。
若是担心那夜里的风急雨寒，
就让我们边走边唱，这路也会变得平缓，
就让我们边走边唱，让我给你减轻负担。

M. 孩子，不要再讲，
等我们把要紧的事情先忙，
最好等他[1]来了，再继续歌唱！

---

[1] 可能指前文提到的Menalcas。

ECLOGA X

Gallus痛失了恋人，倒在地上奄奄一息。这时各色人等都来围观安慰，而Gallus唱出了著名的"爱征服一切"，也唱出了所有人的心声。

ECLOGA X

Extremum hunc, Arethusa[1], mihi concede laborem:

pauca meo Gallo[2], sed quae legat ipsa Lycoris[3],

carmina sunt dicenda neget quis carmina Gallo?

sic tibi, cum fluctus subterlabere Sicanos[4],

5   Doris[5] amara suam non intermisceat undam.

incipe; sollicitos Galli dicamus amores,

dum tenera attondent simae virgulta capellae.

non canimus surdis; respondent omnia silvae.

quae nemora, aut qui vos saltus habuere, puellae

10   Naides[6], indigno cum Gallus amore peribat?

nam neque Parnasi[7] vobis iuga, nam neque Pindi[8]

ulla moram fecere, neque Aoniae[9] Aganippe[10].

illum etiam lauri, etiam flevere myricae.

---

[1] Arethusa是一位nymph妖精，也有说是Diana的随从。她被河神Alpheus 追求，逃至Sicily，所以这里有她代表的同名圣泉。有传言她从大海中流过， 到Sicily岛上现身。

[2] Gallus，即Gaius Cornelius Gallus，作者的朋友，同时代的政治家。参 见VI.64注。

[3] Lycoris似乎是Gallus的情妇，当时著名的女演员。Gallus为她写了四卷 哀歌，但未能存世。

[4] Sicani是古代居住在Tiber河流域的民族，后一部分迁徙至Sicily岛上，这 里指代Sicily岛。

[5] Doris是一位nymph，*Oceanus*与*Tethys*之女，海神Nereus的妻子，前面 水之妖精Galatea的母亲。

[6] Nais，水之妖精，参见II.46。

[7] Parnasus山，参见VI.29。

[8] Pindus山，在希腊中部，也是Muse的圣山。

[9] Aonia地区，在希腊中部，参见VI.65。

[10] Aganippe是Muse圣山Helion上的一处泉水，是Muse的圣泉。Muse也被 称为Aganippids，泉水之女神。

牧歌・其十

Arethusa，请把这最后的苦活交给我：
我要给我的Gallus写首短歌，
让那Lycoris自己念念也不错，
谁会拒绝将Gallus的故事述说？
Arethusa，愿你在Sicilia的激流中穿过，
不要跟Doris那苦涩的海水混合！

开始吧，趁塌鼻的山羊在吃娇嫩的野果[1]，
开始吧，让我们唱起Gallus焦虑的爱火；
我们可不是对牛弹琴[2]——
树林对所有人都会附和！
当Gallus被残忍的爱意折磨，
水仙女们，
你们在何处森林，哪处草坡？
那Parnasus和Pindus的高山，
没有将你们的行程阻拦，
那Aonia的Aganippe圣泉，
也没让你们的脚步放缓。
那月桂也为他伤感，
那柽柳也为他哀叹！

---

[1] 原文是吃灌木丛。
[2] 原文也是类似的成语"对聋唱歌"。

pinifer illum etiam sola sub rupe iacentem

15 Maenalus[1], et gelidi fleverunt saxa Lycaei[2].

stant et oves circum; nostri nec paenitet illas,

nec te paeniteat pecoris, divine poeta;

et formosus ovis ad flumina pavit Adonis[3];

venit et upilio; tardi venere subulci[4];

20 uvidus hiberna venit de glande Menalcas.

omnes 'unde Amor iste' rogant 'tibi?' venit Apollo:

'Galle, quid insanis?' inquit; 'tua cura Lycoris

perque nives alium perque horrida castra secuta est.'

venit et agresti capitis Silvanus[5] honore,

25 florentis ferulas[6] et grandia lilia quassans.

Pan deus Arcadiae venit, quem vidimus ipsi

sanguineis ebuli[7] bacis minioque rubentem.

'ecquis erit modus?' inquit; 'Amor non talia curat;

nec lacrimis crudelis Amor, nec gramina rivis,

30 nec cytiso saturantur apes, nec fronde capellae.'

---

[1]Maenalus山，参见VIII.21。

[2]Lycaeus也是Arcadia的一座山，有Pan神的祭祀活动，常作为Pan神的别名。

[3]希腊神话中的Adonis是他的母亲Myrrha与外祖父乱伦所生，曾被冥后Persephone抚养长大。他异常英俊，是爱神Aphrodite与冥后Persephone的情人，传说他也是Apollo与酒神的男宠。

[4]有版本做bubulci，领着耕牛的耕夫。

[5]Silvanus是荒野的山神，有人也将其等同于Pan神，但是作者一般区别对待二者。他的头上一般装饰着花环，手上拿着柏树。

[6]ferula即Ferula communis，大阿魏。参见V.31注。

[7]ebulus指Sambucus ebulus，一种欧洲南部生长的接骨木，有红色的浆果。

他独自躺在山岩下，奄奄一息，
苍松挺拔的Maenalus山为他哭泣，
寒冷险峻的Lycaeus山为他惋惜！
连羊群也都站在他的周围——
神圣的诗人啊，
羊群不会因为我们羞愧，
你也不要嫌弃羊群卑微！
英俊的Adonis也赶着羊去河边喝水！
牧羊人也来了，懒惰的赶猪人也来了，
还有采收完冬天的橡子[1]，全身湿漉的Menalcas。
他们都在问："你为何落入爱神之手？"
那Apollo也来问："Gallus，何事让你如此疯狂？
你的挚爱Lycoris已经随他人流浪，
穿越冰寒的雪地，穿越残酷的营帐。"
Silvanus也来了，他头上都是山野的芬芳；
盛开的大阿魏和大朵的百合花轻轻摇晃。
那Arcadia的Pan神也来了！
我们都看见他的脸上，
涂着朱砂和接骨木的血色果浆！
他也问道：
"何时才有个尽头，你的哀伤？
爱神才不会关心，你的凄凉！
眼泪满足不了爱神的疯狂，
就如同小溪满足不了草场，
苜蓿花满足不了蜜蜂的窖藏，
苜蓿叶满足不了饿坏的山羊！"

---

[1]冬日收橡子事，见《农事诗》I.305。

tristis at ille: 'tamen cantabitis, Arcades,' inquit
'montibus haec vestris: soli cantare periti
Arcades. o mihi tum quam molliter ossa quiescant,
vestra meos olim si fistula dicat amores!
35 atque utinam ex vobis unus vestrique fuissem
aut custos gregis, aut maturae vinitor uvae!
certe, sive mihi Phyllis, sive esset Amyntas,
seu quicumque furor—quid tum, si fuscus Amyntas;
et nigrae violae[1] sunt et vaccinia[2] nigra—
40 mecum inter salices lenta sub vite iaceret;
serta mihi Phyllis legeret, cantaret Amyntas.
hic gelidi fontes, hic mollia prata, Lycori,
hic nemus; hic ipso tecum consumerer aevo[3].

---

[1]参见II.47注。
[2]参见II.18注。
[3]相对于tempus表示一段的时间，aevum表示无限的时间概念，即永恒，常表示人的一生。

但他忧郁地叹道[1]：

"你们这些Arcadia的眷属[2]啊，

朝着你们的大山歌唱吧！

只有你们Arcadia的眷属擅长歌唱！

噢，倘若有那么一天，

你们的芦笛能传唱我的爱恋，

那我的遗骸也会得到至福的永眠。

然而我真盼着成为你们的一员，

或是驱赶大群山羊的奶鲜，

或是采摘成熟葡萄的香甜！

的确，那样我会有Phyllis的思念，

或是Amyntas的缠绵，

或是其他的热恋！

——噢，Amyntas有点黑又怎样，

就像那香堇花也会带点墨妆，

如同那野山桑更是黑得发亮！

我就在葡萄柔枝下，在柳树间闲躺，

Phyllis给我采来了花环的芳香，

而Amyntas在放声歌唱！

这里，有泉水的冰寒，

这里，有草地的柔软，

噢，Lycoris！

这里，还有森林为伴，

这里，还有我跟你一起，

消磨一生的浪漫。

---

[1]这里下面一大段都是Gallus的回应。

[2]指在场这些歌唱得好的人，如同VII.4的"Arcadia的小伙"。

nunc insanus amor duri me Martis[1] in armis

45   tela[2] inter media atque adversos detinet hostes:

tu procul a patria—nec sit mihi credere tantum!

Alpinas, ah dura, nives et frigora Rheni

me sine sola vides. ah, te ne frigora laedant!

ah, tibi ne teneras glacies secet aspera plantas!

50   ibo, et, Chalcidico[3] quae sunt mihi condita versu

carmina, pastoris Siculi modulabor avena.

certum est in silvis, inter spelaea ferarum

malle pati, tenerisque meos incidere amores

arboribus; crescent illae, crescetis, amores.

55   interea mixtis lustrabo Maenala[4] nymphis,

aut acris venabor apros; non me ulla vetabunt

frigora Parthenios[5] canibus circumdare saltus.

iam mihi per rupes videor lucosque sonantis

ire; libet Partho[6] torquere Cydonia[7] cornu

60   spicula: tamquam haec sit nostri medicina furoris,

aut deus ille malis hominum mitescere discat!

---

[1]Mars，战神。

[2]telum是一种投掷用或者近战用的标枪式武器，可长可短。

[3]Chalcis，在希腊的Euboea岛上，与大陆有一座很短的桥连接。这里指代这里出生的诗人Euphorion。

[4]Maenalus山，参见VIII.21注。

[5]Parthenius山也在Arcadia。

[6]Parthi人，擅长弓箭，参见I.63。

[7]Cydonia是Crete的一座城市，这里指代Crete，也以弓术闻名。

但如今对不幸战神的狂爱将我阻拦，
我在这长矛短枪和凶残的敌人之间纷乱。
你，却远走他乡——我真不敢相信！
啊，你抛下我，狠心的姑娘！
你独自去看Alps山的白雪，Rhine河的严霜，
啊，愿你不要被冰雪所伤！
啊，愿坚冰不要割到你稚嫩的脚掌！
我要用Chalcis的歌辞谱写，
还要用Sicilia的牧笛奏乐！
我心意已决，
在这山林间忍受与兽穴为伍，
把我的爱刻上鲜嫩的树木——
一天一天长大，参天的大树，
一天一天长大，爱情的凄苦[1]！
与此同时，我将与那些nymph女神携手，
走遍Maenalus的山头，
一同狩猎迅捷的野兽[2]；
没有任何寒冷能阻止我带着猎狗，
在Parthenius的森林围狩！
我看到自己，在山岩和回响的林间游荡，
用Parthi人的牛角弓引箭，
让Crete的箭矢飞翔，
真是让人心情舒畅！
惟愿这些能缓解我的相思，
而神明也该学着对苦命之人展现仁慈！

---

[1]原文是"树在长大，爱也在长大"。
[2]原文是野猪。

iam neque Hamadryades[1] rursus nec carmina nobis

ipsa placent; ipsae rursus concedite silvae.

non illum nostri possunt mutare labores,

65   nec si frigoribus mediis Hebrumque[2] bibamus,

Sithoniasque[3] nives hiemis subeamus aquosae,

nec si, cum moriens alta liber aret in ulmo,

Aethiopum[4] versemus ovis sub sidere Cancri[5].

omnia vincit Amor; et nos cedamus Amori.'

70   haec sat erit, divae, vestrum cecinisse poetam,

dum sedet et gracili fiscellam texit hibisco[6],

Pierides; vos haec facietis maxima Gallo—

Gallo, cuius amor tantum mihi crescit in horas,

quantum vere novo viridis se subicit alnus.

75   surgamus; solet esse gravis cantantibus umbra;

iuniperi gravis umbra; nocent et frugibus umbrae.

ite domum saturae, venit Hesperus[7], ite capellae.

---

[1]Hamadryas，指树林的nymph。

[2]Hebrus是Thrace的一条大河。

[3]Sithonii即Thrace人。

[4]即罗马人所知尼罗河的南方，在今Sudan，South Sudan与Ethiopia。

[5]在罗马同纬度的地区，黄道，即太阳的轨道，不会经过天顶。但是在非洲，特别是在罗马人所知非洲最南的国度，北回归线附近，在夏至前后太阳正午经过天顶；而这时太阳在双子宫与巨蟹宫之间，巨蟹宫也会在随之经过天顶，时间大概是午后一点。所以这里是罗马人已知最热的地方，最热的日子和一天中最热的时间点。

[6]药葵，参见II.30注。

[7]即昏星，参见VI.61。昏星不存在"升起"一说，它是在太阳落山或者快落山时在西方天空现身，然后慢慢跟着太阳落入地平线下。

而如今这时代，无论是林中的女孩，
或是歌声的澎湃，都无法让我畅怀，
这森林自己也是无精打采。
让我经历这些苦劳——
让我在严寒的日子去喝Hebrus的河水，
让我去体验Sithonii人多雨冬日的雪堆；
让我在巨蟹座正下去Ethiopia放羊受罪，
边上高挺的榆树，树皮被晒成死灰——
这些苦劳都无法改变那爱情的滋味！
爱征服一切；让我们屈服于爱的光辉！"

神样的Muse啊，
把这些交给你的诗人传唱，
已经足够他用纤细的药葵编个篮筐！
对Gallus而言，你们让这歌更加伟大，
正如绿色的榿木在早春时节吐露新芽，
我对Gallus的爱每时每刻都在增加。
我们该起身了，
黄昏的阴影对歌手不太友好，
刺柏的影子也是沉重的烦恼，
那树影还会损伤果实与谷苞；
该回家了，山羊们已经吃饱[1]，
该回家了，黄昏星已经闪耀。

---

[1] 原文是"吃饱的山羊们，该回家了"。

Translator's Notes and Acknowledgements

There are over twenty mortal characters here, and I personally read this book as a whole, which means the same name always refers to the same mortal character, and the author was composing stories of only one Tityrus, one Menalcas and one Daphnis. Some may find apparent inconsistencies among the poems, but it is not difficult to sort things out once you accept a few principles:

1. When people sing for a competition, they do not necessarily sing their own story.

2. The poems were not chronically ordered.

3. Each character may have different lovers as time changes, and may even have multiple lovers at the same time.

First of all, the "Muses" or the "Pierides": They were first called by Damoetas in III.85 to feed the cows for Pollio. The verb *pasco* may have different meanings, but nothing I can really connect to the real goddesses. The Muses may be happy to accept some sacrifices, but nobody would really ask goddesses to offer cows to a mortal being. So, as a conclusion, these *Pierides* are referring to some sisters in the village, probably whose name appeared in the poems as well. Vergil's *Georgics* is more than two times longer than his *Eclogues*, and guess how many times he used "Pierides" there? Zero. How about the much longer *Aeneid*? Zero.

Well, there aren't many female characters here. Galatea and Amaryllis (I.31) were most likely related since Amaryllis inherited Galatea's slave (Tityrus). Corydon actually had some love affair with both (VII.40, II.14,52) at different times, which could be quite common when you have a neighbor with two or more sisters of similar ages. But at last Corydon chose to marry Amaryllis as he called her "my Amaryllis" (II.52).

Now as the author mentioned, 3 is the number that pleases the gods (VIII.75), there was probably another one, who was holding this magical ritual and asked her sister Amaryllis for help (VIII.77). Some believe that this Amaryllis is a maid of the same name, which of course is possible, but it is more interesting if it is the same Amaryllis. The third (and possibly the youngest) fell in love with Daphnis, who was still alive in VIII (but in town). However, it could be the case that Daphnis was already dead there (as he was definitely dead in V) and she simply had an illusion that a magical ritual can bring him back. Then what she performed was really a ritual to summon the dead. What is her name? This may not be direct from the text, but she may be Phyllis mentioned throughout the book: Corydon talked about her love for hazel-trees as if he cared about Phyllis as well (VII.63).

Three of them are daughters of a local landlord, Iollas (III.76), as Damoetas reminded us about Juppiter and his daughters. The family are friends of the old Damoetas, who called them *Pierides* as an epithet of their beauty and their love of songs, and who gifted his reed-pipe to Corydon (Amaryllis' husband) when he was dying (II.37).

Amyntas loved Damoetas, but the latter was not so keen to their love (II.39, III.74). But Amyntas was also a relatively good singer (V.8), so were most people here, except maybe for Tityrus.

Tityrus was a slave of Damon and Galatea (I.31, III.20), and later Corydon and Amaryllis, from whom he gained freemanship. His singing was not well-celebrated (VIII.55), and Melioebus was surprised to see him playing with his pipe in I.2. His song, VI, is very unrelated to the other part of the story, and is probably the least interesting one among the ten. Instead, most people was looking for Tityrus as a shepherd (III.20, III.96, V.12, IX.23). He is definitely *not* a representation of Vergil himself, but instead some close friend whose real name has lost in the history (see *Georgics* IV.566).

Daphnis was likely the Daphnis in old mythology, son of Mercury, and lived in Sicily (and so the villagers were all in Sicily, which we will later elaborate). A nymph cursed him because she fell in love with him (a similar story as in VIII). He fell off a cliff and died, and people mourned over his early and sudden death as in V (he was a child in III.14). Is this Daphnis a representation of Julius Caesar? I don't think so — because Menalcas once asked Daphnis to look at Caesar's star (XI.47).

Damoetas is likely a character with a big inconsistency. He was dead in II as he had given his pipe to Corydon, and in III he had some argument and a competition with Menalcas, which happened years before II, which is still consistent. But in V.84, Menalcas mentioned that he used his pipe to sing both II and III, which seems to imply that Damoetas was already dead in V, but in V.72 he also mentioned that he wanted Damoetas and Aegon to sing songs during a biannual festival or sacrifice in honor of Daphnis.

So one explanation is that, V.84 was in fact a different song, or maybe an earlier version of II, when Damoetas was still alive. The reason is, Corydon was singing this love song alone to the forests and the mountains (II.4), and so Menalcas would have no access to it, as long as Corydon did not embarrass himself. So while everyone knows Corydon fell in love with Alexis, people made songs about it and Menalcas probably was talking about his own version, and as you may imagine, Menalcas wouldn't be very happy singing about himself as a potential-lover with Corydon and being complained of his own skin color (II.15-16).

Yet another explanation is that, V.56-80 was a song from a distant past compared to V itself, when Daphnis had died but Damoetas was still alive. This was also indicated in V.55 as Stimichon talked about it long time ago.

Damon and Corydon were the "poets of Pierides". Corydon was also good at interweaving baskets (II.72), and in the end (X.71) Gallus also recalled such skills of "Muses' poet". Menalcas, a potential lover of Corydon, was also good at singing (IX.10), but he was likely older than Corydon and younger than the old Damoetas. Galatea as a young girl loved Menalcas (III.64,72), but Menalcas preferred the young Tityrus (III.69, see also I.58 *palumbes*), and so in the end Galatea married Damon and Tityrus was their slave.

Mopsus was younger than Menalcas as well (V.4). He had sung stories of Phyllis, Alcon and Codrus (V.10-11), and Menalcas believed he was better than Amyntas (who was not so talented as Corydon in II.39). but he committed suicide (VIII) which happened after Daphnis' sudden death (V). So this leads to another seeming inconsistency: Mopsus was dead in VIII but Daphnis was still alive.

Well, one possibility is that, in VIII, Alphesiboeus was singing a song which had been composed long time ago, even before Mopsus' death. Or, as I mentioned earlier, it could be the case that Daphnis was already dead in the song, and the girl, possibly Phyllis, was having an illusion that Daphnis was travelling to the city instead, and so she had to use magical powers and was questioning her senses in the end. The reigniting ashes (VIII.105) also indicated the resurrection of the dead.

The ceremony she asked Amaryllis to perform — throwing ashes over one's head — recalled the story of Deucalion and Pyrrha (VI.41) of the new generation humans, also indicated a sense of resurrection.

Where were these people living? I think the answer is Sicily, despite a few misleading hints for Mantua, Vergil's hometown. Meliboeus was mentioning the bees from Hybla (I.55); Corydon talked about his lambs wondering around Sicilian mountains (II.21) and looked at his own image in the sea (II.26). In IV, the poet called the "Sicilian Muses", which could also mean the Pierides sisters. Thalia came to play with Syracuse's songs in VI.1. The sea-nymphs Galatea (who is different from the oldest of the sisters) and Arethusa also reminded people about the current location as well.

In VII, Meliboeus was mentioning Arcadia and Mincius at the same time, which indicated that these locations could be fictitious (see VII.13). Moreover, Bianor's tomb in IX.60 seems to indicate that they were in Mantua, but Ocnus (Bianor), as a minor character in mythology, founded a few other cities as well, and there is no record of him being buried in Mantua. He was said to spend eternity in Tartarus.

——◦⌒◦——

Back to the translation: I finished translating *the Eclogues* much earlier than expected, maybe because I had already had my painstaking experience working through *the Georgics*. It has been a much smoother work-flow: parsing Latin, making footnotes and indices, brainstorming word choices and rhyming the lines; and I don't have much to worry about caring cattle or bees, or grape vines, or ploughing, or varieties of olives. But I was questioning myself all along the way: How do we make translations more *poetic*?

Let the time arrow reverse to the moment when I was translating, or struggling through *the Georgics*, Book III, line 338, which reads as:

> *litoraque alcyonem resonant, acalanthida dumi.*

Oh my god! This is beautiful! Parsing Latin had been very much pain, and I didn't even understand what kind of creature *acalanthis* is, but the final *"lan-thi-da/du-mi"* was like a breeze during a hot summer day, or a clear fountain pouring out fresh water for the dying grass.

I suddenly realized why this work has resisted the inevitable erosion of time.

You may think it is the meter that helps to make a poem here, but I argue that the meter serves rather as a restraint, so that Vergil had to remove the verb from *acalanthida dumi*, but now you can put in all kinds of verbs by yourself! What does thorn-bush do to a little bird? I don't know, but this is the real fun part.

So my point is, *restraints are more interesting*. With limited word choices, it makes it more challenging to pick a perfect one to express the idea. The same thing happened to me when I tried to rhyme along the lines — I had to run through the "rhyming table" to find appropriate characters, and sometimes rephrase almost the entire line to make things fit. This also generated a number of expressions that I have never thought about, making things a bit more poetic in my opinion.

Another way of keeping a restraint is to limit the line numbers in agreement with the original, as some other translators did; or to keep six ideas or grammatical units within one line, to mimic a dactylic hexameter. It is just a personal preference, in my opinion.

Speaking of other translations, I would like to give thanks to the following:

- 牧歌, by Yang Xianyi, 1957
- 牧歌, by Dang Cheng, 2016
- 牧歌集, by Zhai Wentao, on Dickinson Classics Online
- 牧歌, by Mu et al., on reeds.com.cn
- *The Eclogues of Virgil*, by David Ferry, 1999
- *Eclogues*, by James B. Greenough, 1895

If you ask me, why did I decide to translate *the Eclogues* as there are four (and a few more translated from English) translations available?

First of all, I would like to give readers a consistent taste following my translation of *the Georgics*, as well as a different taste from previous works by other translators.

Secondly, I would like to share my humble understanding the text, especially in a slightly different way compared to classical interpretations. It does not change much of the translation, but it generates more fun.

Finally and most importantly, I am addicted to the cover design, side by side with *the Georgics*. There, the golden color represents the agricultural themes: grains, grapes and olive oil, hay-stalks and leather, bees and honey, and harvests of labor. Here, everything is green: pastures, forests, leaf-beds and ways of life.

Index

Achilles, 52, 54
Acis, 92
Adonis, 128
Adriatic, 100
Aegle, 76
Aegon, 30, 68
Aeneas, 120
Afer, 12
Aganippe, 126
Alceus, 94
Alcimedon, 34
Alcippe, 88
Alcon, 60, 90
Alexis, 18, 70, 94
Alphesiboeus, 68, 100
Alpheus, 126
Alps, 132
Amaryllis, 18, 24, 32, 42, 108,
     110, 118
Amphion, 20
Amyntas, 22, 40, 42, 60, 62,
     130
Antevorta, 38
Antigenes, 70
Antiope, 20

Aonia, 82, 126
Aphrodite, *see* Venus
Apollo, 24, 38, 40, 46, 50, 56,
     60, 64, 68, 74, 76,
     82, 84, 90, 94, 128
Aracynthus, 20
Arar, 12
Arcadia, 56, 88, 90, 102, 128,
     132
Archimedes, 36
Arethusa, 126
Argo, 54, 78
Ariadne, 78
Arion, 106
Ariusium, 68
Armenia, 62
Artemis, *see* Diana
Ascra, 82
Assyria, 52
Astraea, 50
Athena, *see* Minerva
Athens, 20, 25
Attica, 20
Augustus, 100, 118, 120
Auster, 24, 70

Bacchus, 62, 68, 74, 78, 90,
      94, 128
Bavius, 44
Bianor, 122
Boeotia, 20
Boreas, 92
Britanni, 12

Caesar, 118, 120
Calliope, 56
Camenae, 38
Cancer, 134
Carmenta, 38
Castalia, 76
Caucasus, 78
Ceres, 68
Chalcis, 132
Chaonia, 116
Chios, 68
Chromis, 74
Cinna, 118
Circe, 108
Codrus, 60, 90
Conon, 36
Corsica, 118
Cortyna, 80
Corydon, 18, 32, 70, 88, 116
Cremona, 118
Crete, 12, 68, 78, 80, 132
Cronus, *see* Saturnus
Cumae, 50
Cupido, 104
Cydonia, 132
Cynthius, *see* Apollo
Cynthus, 74
Cyplops, 92
Cyrons, 118

Damoetas, 22, 30, 68, 90
Damon, 32, 100
Daphnis, 20, 32, 62, 64, 88
Dardanus, 24
Delia, *see* Diana
Delos, 40, 74
Delphi, 76
Demeter, *see* Ceres
Demica, *see* Parcae
Deucalion, 78
Diana, 40, 50, 90, 126
Dicte, 80
Dione, 120
Dionysus, *see* Bacchus
Dirce, 20
Dodona, 6, 116
Doris, 126
Dryadas, 66
Dulichium, 82

Emathides, 42
Eratosthenes, 36
Ethiopia, 134
Euboea, 132
Euphorion, 132
Europa, 80
Eurotas, 84
Eurydice, 36

Faunus, *see* Pan

Gaia, 78, 110, 120

Galatea, 32, 40, 92, 126
Gallus, 82, 126
Garamantes, 104
Germania, 12
Grynium, 82

Hamadryas, 134
Hebrus, 134
Helion, 82, 126
Helios, 78, 80, 104
Hera, *see* Juno
Hercules, 78, 94, 102
Hermes, *see* Mercury
Hesiod, 82
Hesperus, *see* Vesper
Hybla, 10, 92
Hylas, 78
Hylas, a dog, 112

Iacchus, *see* Bacchus
Ida, 24
Illyrii, 100
Iollas, 24, 42
Ismarus, 76
Ithaca, 82

Jason, 54, 104
Juno, 50, 80
Juppiter, 6, 20, 38, 76, 78, 80,
        94, 116

Liber, *see* Bacchus

Libethra, 90
Libya, 104
Linus, 56, 82
Lucifer, 80, 102
Lucina, 50
Luna, 108
Lycaeus, 128
Lycidas, 94, 116
Lycisca, 32
Lycoris, 126, 130
Lyctus, 68

Maenalus, 102, 128, 132
Maevius, 44
Mantua, 118, 122
Mars, 116, 132
Medea, 104
Melampus, 78
Meliboeus, 4, 30, 70, 88
Menalcas, 18, 30, 60, 116,
        118, 123, 128
Mercury, 20
Micon, 30, 90
Mincius, 88
Minerva, 24
Minos, 78
Minotaur, 78
Mnasyllos, 74
Moeris, 110, 116
Mopsus, 60, 102
Morta, *see* Parcae
Muse, 4, 38, 42, 50, 56, 70,
        74, 76, 82, 88, 90,
        100, 106, 118, 126,
        134
Myrrha, 128

Nais, 22, 76, 126
Neaera, 30
Neptune, 78
Nereus, 78, 92, 126
Nisa, 102
Nisus, 82
Nona, *see* Parcae
Nyx, 80

Oaxes, 12
Oceanus, 78, 120, 126
Odysseus, 82, 108
Oeagrus, 56
Oeta, 102
Olympus, 66, 84
Orpheus, 36, 56, 76, 90, 106

Palaemon, 36
Pales, 64
Pallas, *see* Minerva
Pan, 20, 56, 66, 76, 102, 108,
    128
Parcae, 54
Paris, 24
Parnasus, 76, 126
Parthenius, 132
Parthi, 12, 132
Pasiphae, 78
Peloponnese, 56
Permessus, 82
Perse, 78
Persephone, 128
Phaethon, 80
Philomela, 84

Phoebus, *see* Apollo
Phosphorus, *see* Lucifer
Phyllis, 42, 46, 60, 88, 90, 94,
    130
Pierides, 42, 74, 106, 118,
    134
Pindus, 126
Poeni, 62
Pollio, 42, 44, 50, 100
Polyphemus, 92
Pontus, 110
Poseidon, *see* Neptune
Postvorta, 38
Priapus, 90
Procne, 84
Proetus, 78
Prometheus, 78
Pyrrha, 78

Rhea, 80
Rhine, 132
Rhodope, 76, 104

Saturnus, 50, 78, 80
Scylla, 82
Scythia, 12
Selene, *see* Luna
Sicani, 126
Sicilia, 20, 74, 92, 126, 132
Siculi, *see* Sicilia
Silenus, 74
Silvanus, 128
Sithonii, 134
Sophocles, 100
Sparta, 84
Stimichon, 66

Syracuse, 74
Syrinx, 20

Tereus, 84
Tethys, 78, 120, 126
Thalia, 70, 74
Thebes, 20
Thestylis, 18, 22
Thetis, 52
Thrace, 56, 76, 84, 134
Thyrsis, 88, 116
Tiber, 126
Tigris, 12
Timavus, 100
Tiphys, 54
Tityrus, 4, 32, 44, 60, 74,
        106, 118
Tmaros, 104
Troia, 24

Ulixes, *see* Odysseus
Urania, 56
Uranus, 120

Varius, 118
Varus, 74, 118
Venus, 24, 40, 94, 104, 120,
        128
Vesper, 80, 84, 102, 134
Virgo, *see* Astraea

Zephyr, 60
Zethus, 20
Zeus, *see* Juppiter

www.ingramcontent.com/pod-product-compliance
Lightning Source LLC
Chambersburg PA
CBHW030305130626
46549CB00002B/712